The Private Library
What We Do Know, What We Don't Know, What We Ought to Know About Our Books

Arthur Lee Humphreys

Alpha Editions

This edition published in 2024

ISBN 9789362517616

Design and Setting By
Alpha Editions
www.alphaedis.com
Email - info@alphaedis.com

As per information held with us this book is in Public Domain.
This book is a reproduction of an important historical work.
Alpha Editions uses the best technology to reproduce historical work
in the same manner it was first published to preserve its original nature.
Any marks or number seen are left intentionally to preserve.

Contents

PREFACE	- 1 -
What is a Good Edition?	- 2 -
What is a Fine Copy?	- 4 -
Book Values.	- 6 -
On the Care of Books.	- 9 -
The Art of Reading.	- 14 -
Common-place Books.	- 20 -
Reference Books.	- 21 -
Boudoir Libraries.	- 23 -
Bookbinding.	- 26 -
Book Hobbies.	- 31 -
Old Country Libraries.	- 33 -
Weeding Out.	- 37 -
The Catalogue.	- 38 -
Classification of Books.	- 41 -
Bookcases.	- 44 -
Miscellaneous Appliances.	- 48 -
The Library Annexe.	- 50 -
A Librarian.	- 53 -
The Library Architecturally.	- 55 -
Munificent Book-buying.	- 61 -
PASSAGES ILLUSTRATIVE OF THE FOREGOING.	- 63 -
The Medici and their Friends.	- 64 -
The Dukes of Urbino.	- 68 -

Pieresc.	- 71 -
Mr. Ruskin's Advice.	- 72 -
FOOTNOTES:	- 73 -

PREFACE

WITH *all the literature published on behalf of Free Libraries—institutions which, after all, are of doubtful good—no one so far has written a book to assist in making* THE PRIVATE LIBRARY *combine practical useful qualities with decorative effect.*

For many years I have had opportunities of inspecting and reporting upon Collections of Books in numerous Country Houses, and I must say that the condition of books in the greater number of them is chaotic. A man will talk about all his possessions—his pictures, his objets d'art, his horses, his garden, and his bicycle, but rarely will he talk about his books; and if he does so, all his geese are swans, or just as often, all his swans are geese. There are servants in every house qualified to do everything except handle a book. There is no reason why the Library should not be just as much a place[vi] of amusement as the billiard-room, where the men are usually to be found. Books are much more amusing than billiards, and you may learn to play in jest or work in earnest with books just as you take to any other amusement. The whole truth is that at present books do not get a proper share of attention, and it is with the desire to remedy such a condition of things that I have printed this little volume, containing things that we do know, that we don't know, and that we ought to know about our books.

A. L. H.

187 PICCADILLY, W.

[vii]

What is a Good Edition?

A good edition should be a complete edition, ungarbled and unabridged. If the author is a classic, the *format* of the copy chosen should in some way represent the style of the author. *Gibbon*, for instance, should be in large octavo or quarto, with print of a size to correspond. This is not always possible, for English editions of books often aim at mere cheapness, and of many great authors there exist no good editions. Thus there is no suitable edition of the classics printed in England, as there is and for long has been in France. A good edition is not necessarily an expensive edition, nor is it necessarily noble and generous in print and margin. The editions known as the 'Globe'[2] editions of Pope and others are good editions because (1) They are complete; (2) Each one has been taken in hand and superintended by the most competent scholar and has notes sufficient but not pedantic; (3) Because they are well printed on paper of fair quality by printers who give wages liberally to careful press readers; (4) Because each work being a work of the first or classic order, it is bound in a simple and unaffected style, without meretricious gold or tawdry ornament. Now the 'Globe' editions are fitting in their place as types of right editions of the cheap kind. I will now take right editions of the more liberal and expensive kind. The 'Cambridge' *Shakespeare*, the last issue, each play in a separate volume, is right because (1) The print, paper, spacing, and simplicity of binding, are suited to the dignity of the work; (2) The edition has had brought to it fulness of knowledge and rightness of judgment; (3) Each volume is light to handle and easy to hold, and flexible in opening.

But it would be misleading to say that these are the only examples of right editions. In other books which I might name, excellent[3] work has been brought to play which in the two types already named there was not scope for. I would like therefore to take another instance, and name the editions of Pope's *Works*, edited by Courthope and Elwin, of Walpole's *Letters*, edited by Peter Cunningham, and Boswell's *Johnson*, edited by Birkbeck Hill. These editions contain excellent and workmanlike features, such as good arrangement and good indexing, with notes and elucidations sufficiently ample. The size too of each volume is not extravagant as in certain *éditions de luxe*. Now in order that we may have good editions, there are, at least, ten people who must work well together: (1) the Author, (2) the Publisher, (3) the Printer, (4) the Reader, (5) the Compositor, (6) the Pressman, (7) the Paper Maker, (8) the Ink Maker, (9) the Bookbinder, (10) the Consumer.[1] When these ten people are not working in harmony, a book is spoilt. Too often the author, without technical knowledge of book production, insists on certain whims and fancies of his own being carried out. Too often the publisher aims at cheapness and nothing more.

[4]

The publications issued by Pickering in the 'forties' and 'fifties' were models of good workmanship. Pickering published and Whittingham printed, and it was their custom to first sit in consultation upon every new book, and painfully hammer out each in his own mind its ideal form and proportions. Then two Sundays at least were required to compare notes in the little summer house in Mr. Whittingham's garden at Chiswick. Here they would discuss size and quality of paper, the shape of the printed page, the number of lines, the size of the type, the form and comeliness of the title-page.[2] In all technical details the *Edinburgh* edition of R. L. Stevenson's works is satisfying. Here are more 'lines of beauty' than in almost any other modern printed book. As we handle it we feel *satisfied* that it *is right*. Perhaps it was such a *format* that Mr. Ruskin had in mind when he shaped out a scheme of a Royal series of books, which should be models of good work all round. And though it is necessary that we have cheap editions, and that books should circulate everywhere, we want to save the book trade from shoddy work by keeping good models before[5] us. That we produce the best thought in the best form, and not in any mean, shabby dress, ought indeed to be a serious aim of everybody engaged in the matter.

What is a Fine Copy?

To judge of a fine copy requires some years' handling of books. To some, the school prize, in light brown calf, represents an ideal of book beauty; to others, a padded binding and round corners. But these are neither beautiful nor in any way fine copies. The school prize book is not a fine copy (1) Because it is bound in a very perishable leather; (2) Because its margins have been trimmed away and ploughed into; (3) Because it is received in a form which renders it impossible to stamp one's own individuality upon it; (4) It has gaudy and meaningless ornaments stamped down the back. The padded binding is impossible as a fine copy because it has had applied to it a wholly incongruous method of preservation. Books require to be clothed, but not to be upholstered. The round corners usually adopted by the upholster[6] binder can claim no advantage, and they rob the book of its natural neatness and squareness of edge. School prize bindings and padded bindings are sins against the sanctity of common sense. What then is a fine copy? Almost, though not entirely, essential is it that it be in the original binding as put out by the publisher, whether it be a paper covering, or cloth, or boards. The reason for this is that in securing a book in such a condition one has the book *in full measure*, and there is no necessity to undo anything which has already been done. Now, if a book be bought in a leather binding, the chances are that it is a leather binding which in no way suits its new owner, and he therefore has not only to sacrifice the binding, but in rebinding it he must sacrifice some of the margins too. The novels of Scott and Marryat in their original boards are delightful to handle. A fine copy should be a clean copy free from spots. When a book is spotted it is called 'foxed,' and these 'foxey' books are for the most part books printed in the early part of this century, when paper-makers first discovered that they could bleach their rags,[7] and, owing to the inefficient means used to neutralise the bleach, the book carried the seeds of decay in itself, and when exposed to any damp soon became discoloured with brown stains.[3] A foxed book cannot have the fox marks removed, and such a book should be avoided. Ink marks can be removed, and a name written upon a title-page can generally be entirely obliterated without leaving any sign that it has been there. Here let me beg people who give presents of books never to write upon title-pages, but upon the fly-leaf. Many thousands of beautiful and valuable volumes are annually ruined for ever by their owners cutting the name from the title. A cut title-page is irreparable. A fine copy may be a bound copy, in which case the edges must not have been cut down, though the top edge may have been gilded, and the binding must be appropriate and not provincial in appearance. A provincial binding lacks finish, the board used is too thick or too thin, or not of good quality, and the leather not properly pared down and turned in. All such things go to spoil good books. In North's *Lives of the Norths* there is a passage[8] which well describes the man of judgment in books. Dr. John North, whose life forms part of this work, is most picturesquely described in his book-loving habits. 'He courted, as a fond lover, all best editions, fairest characters, best bound and preserved. If the subject were in his favour (as the Classics), he cared not how many of them he had, even of the same edition, if he thought it among the best, *rather better bound, squarer cut, neater covers, or some such qualification caught him.*' And then his biographer adds, what is so true, and especially of books, 'Continual use gives men a judgment of things comparatively, and they come to fix on what is most proper and easy, which no man upon cursory view would determine.'

Large paper copies are not necessarily fine copies. When a cheap trumpery piece of book-making is printed on hand-made paper or Japanese vellum paper the result is vulgarity, just as when a common person attempts to swagger about in fine clothes. No, a book must show good binding and be appropriately apparelled, or it cannot be referred to as a fine copy. In the matter of large paper copies[9] it is necessary to form a separate judgment in each case. One thing is certain, that the man who collects large paper books as large paper books is a vulgarian and a fool. He who collects such large paper books as mature judgment determines are appropriate, and because he sees them to have genuine points of merit over and above small paper copies, is a book lover. In a charming little volume, written by an American bibliophile, I read the following passage, confirming in part the foregoing:—

'Good editions of good books, though they may often be expensive, cannot be too highly commended. One can turn to a page in inviting letterpress so much easier than to a page of an unattractive volume.'[4]

Book Values.

It would be impossible to tell all the causes which go towards determining the value of a book and which cause it to fluctuate in price. There is but one way to arrive at a reliable knowledge of book values, and that is to begin stall-hunting as soon as you leave school[10] or college and continue until past middle age, absorbing information from stalls, from catalogues, and from sale-rooms. The records of prices at which books have been sold in the auction rooms, and which are regularly issued, are useless in the hands of an inexperienced person. To make up your mind on Monday that you are going to begin a career of successful bargain-hunting and book-collecting is only to be defrauded on all the other five remaining days. Experience must be bought, and an eye for a good copy of a book, or for a bargain of any kind, only comes after years of practice. I admit that if a man begins collecting some particular class of books, say Angling books, he may sooner arrive at safe judgment alone; but even here he has a pretty wide field to make blunders in. When Gabriel Naudé wrote his pamphlet, *Avis pour dresser une Bibliothèque*, he laid down his first rule thus:—'The first means is to take the counsel and advice of such as are able to give it *viva voce*.' This was written more than two hundred years ago, and still no better advice could possibly be given to a book collector. By all means find a man[11] whom you can trust, and whose knowledge is ample, and stick to him. Do not yourself bid in the auction room, or you will soon find out your mistake. Place your list of wants and your list of commissions in the hands of one good man whom you have reason to trust, and you will then get your money's worth.

I have said that it is impossible to set down all the causes which affect the prices of books, but in an old French bibliographical book, by D. Clement,[5] the subject is gone into more minutely than it has ever since been treated. First, there are causes which may be classed under the heading of *Rarity*. Secondly, there are causes which must be grouped under the head *Condition*.

According to Clement, there are two sorts of rarity in books; the one absolute, the other conditional or contingent. There are rare editions of very common books. There are books of almost common occurrence in public libraries, which are rarely seen in the market. A book or an edition of which but very few copies exist is called 'necessarily rare;' one[12] which is only with difficulty to be met with—however many copies may be extant—he calls 'contingently rare.'

Under the first head he classes; (1) Books of which few copies were printed; (2) Books which have been suppressed; (3) Books which have been almost entirely destroyed by casual fire, or other accident; (4) Books of which a large portion of the impression has been wasted—usually for want of success when published; (5) Volumes of which the printing was never completed; (6) Copies on large paper or on vellum.

Under the second head, he enumerates; (1) Books on subjects which interest only a particular class of students; (2) Books in languages which are little known; (3) Heretical, licentious, and libellous books; (4) First editions of a classic author from MS.; (5) First productions of the printing press in a particular town; (6) The productions of the celebrated printers of the sixteenth century; (7) Books in the vernacular language of an author who printed them in a foreign country; (8) Books privately printed; (9) Works, the various parts of which have been published under different titles, in different sizes, or in various places.[13]

Clement then analyses the degrees of rarity thus: (1) Every book, which is no longer current in the trade, and requires some pains in the search for it, is 'of infrequent occurrence;' (2) If there are but few copies in the country in which we live, and those not easily met with, it is 'rare;' (3) If the copies are so dispersed that there are but few of them, even in the neighbouring countries, so that there is increased difficulty to procure them, it is 'very rare;' (4) If the number of copies be but fifty or sixty, and those scattered, it is 'extremely rare;' (5) And finally, every work of which there are not ten copies in the world is 'excessively rare.' In all these cases, it must be supposed that the book is a book sought for, and that the seekers are more numerous than the sought.[6]

In the matter of *Condition* and its effect upon price, long training is required before all the qualities of a copy can be properly defined. There are copies on 'vellum,' 'large paper,' 'fine paper,' 'coloured paper.' There are 'crisp' copies, 'uncut' copies, 'tall' copies, 'ruled' copies, and 'illustrated' copies, *cum multis aliis*.[7]

[14]

Fashion determines much as to price. As soon as it becomes a fad to collect books relating to some particular subject, competition instantly steps in, and prices go up. It may be well to state, for the benefit of a very numerous and uninitiated public, that, *because a book is old, it is not necessarily rare*. There are many thousands of people who have most imperfect and valueless books, mostly on theology, or some controversial abominations, and these people spend days wasting their own and booksellers' time in seeking to sell at prices which their own imagination alone has determined is right. Distrust the advertisements of large paper editions. *Very* few of them are worth purchasing, and very few, indeed, increase in value. Fight against the first-edition craze, which is the maddest craze that ever affected book collecting. Again and again it must be repeated, and cannot be gainsaid, that *a first edition may be the best, but in most cases it is the worst.* In every case, inquire and find out which is the *best* edition as to completeness, good paper and print, and safe editing, if such has been necessary, and then purchase[15] a copy of that edition. One remark finally. The prices of *all good books* are going up, and any one who lays out money with care within the next ten years will have the enjoyment of his library and a good investment as well.

On the Care of Books.

The two things most neglected in houses are the trimming of lamps and the care of the books. The condition of many libraries in large country houses is most lamentable. In such neglect are they that it would take months, and in some cases years, working day and night, to restore them to a healthy condition. For, poor things! they are really so neglected, that their covers become like the limbs of rheumatic people. If you touch them they seem to shriek and cry with pain. They are either parched for lack of a proper atmosphere, or else they are sticking together with the damp or thickly covered with dust.[8] There is nothing else in a house like this, and why are these things so? It is because there are[16] so few people who understand the care of books. I once read the following in a daily paper, and thought I recognised in it a familiar hand, that of Mr. Andrew Lang:—

'The foes of books are careless people—first of all. They tear pages open with their thumbs, or cut them with sharp knives which damage the margins. It is so difficult to keep paper knives, and ivory paper knives are the favourite pasture of some scholars, who bite the edges till the weapon resembles a dissipated saw. To avoid this temptation some employ mediæval daggers, or skene dhus, but the edges spoil a book. Cigarette ashes are very bad for books, so is butter, also marmalade. Dr. Johnson and Wordsworth are said to have been very careless with their books. Dr. Johnson used to clean his from dust by knocking them together, as Mr. Leighton says housemaids do. Scott was very careful; he had a number of wooden dummies made, and, when a volume was borrowed, he put the dummy in its place on the shelf, inscribing it with the name of the borrower. He also defended his shelves with locked brazen wires. "Tutus clausus ero" ("I[17] shall be safe if shut up"), his anagram, was his motto, under a portcullis. Borrowers, of course, are nearly the worst enemies of books, always careless, and very apt to lose one volume out of a set. Housemaids are seldom bibliophiles. Their favourite plan is to dust the books in the owner's absence, and then rearrange them on fancy principles, mostly upside down. One volume of *Grote* will be put among French novels, another in the centre of a collection on sports, a third in the midst of modern histories, while others are "upstairs and downstairs, and in my lady's chamber." The diversity of sizes, from folio to duodecimo, makes books very difficult to arrange where room is scanty. Modern shelves in most private houses allow no room for folios, which have to lie, like fallen warriors, on their sides.'

All that is very true, particularly about housemaids. Indeed, I have rarely found any woman who cared sufficiently for her books to really fondly tend them.

The principal enemy which books have is DAMP. This means ruination, more perhaps to the paper than to the binding,[18] though both suffer. A fungus growth comes on the leather, and inside there come stains and 'fox' marks. Damp is caused (1) through lack of fires or warmth; (2) through too many sides of a room being exposed to the elements without having the walls battened; (3) the thaw following a frost, proper means for warmth not being adopted during the frost. The only remedy for damp is the trying process of opening each volume and suspending it open, after wiping with a dry cloth each page affected. The next worst enemies are gas and heat.

Gas alone, provided the books are not placed high up, will not be nearly so destructive as it is generally supposed; but all atmospheres heated too highly are destructive. Mr. Poole, a very experienced American librarian, has reported as follows, and, I think, very rightly:—

'The burning of many gas lights doubtless has a tendency to increase the evil by increasing the heat. Yet the deterioration of bindings goes on in the libraries where gas is never used. This fact shows that the chief injury arises from heat, and not merely[19] from the sulphurous residuum of gas combustion.'

Mr. Poole made an experiment in the upper gallery of a library, and found that—

'While the temperature of the floor was 65° Fahr., that of the upper gallery was found to be 142°. Such a temperature dries up the oil of the leather, and burns out its life. Books cannot live where men cannot live.' Similarly, Mr. Blades wrote in his little manual:

'The surest way to preserve your books is to treat them as you would your own children, who are sure to sicken if confined in an atmosphere which is impure, too hot, too cold, too damp, or too dry. It is just the same with the progeny of literature.'

In London particularly dust, smoke, and soot get at books and do great damage. To have the top edges gilded is an excellent way to prevent dust getting into the leaves. Books which have roughly trimmed tops harbour dust much more readily, and it is with great difficulty removed from such. If a book is very dusty, a small brush is perhaps the best means to adopt to remove the offending particles. Books should not be either swung together[20] or beaten together. The carpet in a library should not reach to the wall, or right to the cases, but should fall short so as to be removed when required to be cleaned. A librarian at Bath gives the following advice:—

'Our books are taken down once a year, in the month of August, to be dusted, and, for the last four or five years, I have adopted a simple plan. When the books are well dusted I take about half an ounce of the best horn glue, and, having dissolved it in the usual way, I add to it about a pint of warm water and a teaspoonful of glycerine, and stir it well. Then dipping a soft sponge into the solution, I wash over the backs of the books. If the leather is much perished or decayed, it will unduly absorb the size, and a second touch over may be necessary. The glycerine will have the effect of preventing the glue from drying too hard or stiffening the leather. When dry, the books may be rubbed over with a chamois leather. The above process, I find, helps to nourish the leather, and to restore that property which the heated air has destroyed. It also freshens up and greatly improves the appearance of the volumes upon the shelves.[21] The operation must be repeated once a year at least.'

Bottles of preparation are sold ready made up for this purpose. Mr. Blades warmly echoed the sentiment that housemaids and helps are seldom bibliophiles, and, if, peradventure, one Eve in a family can be indoctrinated with book reverence, there may be salvation for all the books. Mr. Blades himself had a fine library, and goes fully into the subject of the period of dusting and its methods.[9]

'Books *must* now and then be taken down out of their shelves, but they should be tended lovingly and with judgment. If the dusting can be done just outside the room, so much the better. The books removed, the shelf should be lifted quite out of its bearings, cleansed, and wiped, and then each volume should be taken separately and gently rubbed on back and edges with a soft cloth. In returning the volumes to their places, notice should be taken of the binding, and especially when the books are in whole calf or morocco, care should be taken not to let them rub together. The best-bound books are soonest injured, and[22] generally deteriorate in bad company. Certain volumes, indeed, have evil tempers, and will scratch the faces of all their neighbours who are too familiar with them. Such are books with metal clasps and rivets on their edges; and such, again, are those abominable old rascals, chiefly born in the fifteenth century, who are proud of being dressed in real boards with brass corners, and pass their lives with fearful knobs and metal bosses. . . . . When your books are being dusted, don't impute too much common sense to your assistants—take their ignorance for granted.'

Mr. Blades then points out certain dangers which beset the inexperienced handler of books. Never lift a book by one of its corners. Do not pile books up too high. Be careful not to rub the dust *into* instead of *off* the edges. If mildew or damp is discovered, carefully wipe it away, and let the book stand open for some days in a very dry spot—but not in front of a fire. Be careful that no grit is on the duster, or it will surely mark your books. Do not wedge books in too tightly. Common-sense must dictate what is right, but every volume should *fit easily* in its place.[23]

Children and servants are not to be classed as friendly to books, but little lapses on their part are much more easily tolerated than the ignorance of the person who ought to know better. Such people insist upon having their books bound in hideous bindings, and mutilated almost beyond recognition by the bookbinder's plough.

I will talk about bookbinding later, but this I will say, that in no way can a book be easier ruined than by being placed unconditionally in the hands of a bookbinder.

It is frequently supposed that the insect, known as the bookworm, is a great enemy to books. 'Tis true where the bookworm exists it does irreparable damage, but fortunately it is not an insect which may be found every day. In America, they have, I believe, greater trouble from these boring insects. They have 'fish bugs,' 'silver fish,' and 'bustle tails,' scientifically known as *Lepisma Saccharina*. Another is known as 'Buffalo Bug,' or 'Carpet Bug,' or the *Anthrenus varius* of scientists. A third is *Blatta Australasia*, a species of cockroach.

The following maxims may be learned by heart, or if preferred, they can be bought by experience:[24]

Do not bite your paper knife until it has the edge of a saw.

Do not cut books except with a proper ivory paper knife.

It is ruination to a good book not to cut it right through into the corners.

Do not turn the leaves of books down. Particularly, do not turn down the leaves of books printed on plate paper.

If you are in the habit of lending books, do not mark them. These two habits together constitute an act of indiscretion.

It is better to give a book than to lend it.

Never write upon a title-page or half-title. The blank fly-leaf is the right place.

Books are neither card-racks, crumb-baskets, or receptacles for dead leaves.

Books were not meant as cushions, nor were they meant to be toasted before a fire.

Valets and maids appear to take kindly to the packing of everything except books. I will therefore say that only small quantities (twelve volumes to twenty) should be packed in a parcel. Boxes, either wine-cases, or boxes specially made, should be used. Books being very solid and heavy should be[25] packed in strong cases, and the method of packing them should be to place them upright alternately on back and edge in layers. By this means they can be fitted tightly to the case they are meant to travel in. Leather bound volumes should be wrapped up singly before being packed, and the box should be carefully lined with paper so that any roughness on the wood of the box may not damage the volumes.

Book and parcel post volumes should have three or four thicknesses of paper, and if bound volumes a strawboard on either side as well as paper.

The Art of Reading.

First, how to read. The reason why so many people who read much know so little, is because they read isolated books instead of reading one book in connexion with another. The memory is trained by association, and if you read two books in succession on one subject you know more than twice as much as if you had read one book only. A good memory is a[26] memory which assimilates. Every one has a good memory for something. A good memory rejects and sifts, and does not accept everything offered to it like a pillar-box. Do not join reading societies, because they kill individuality. Choose your subject, and work all round it. There is an extensive literature on the subject of 'The Art of Reading,' 'The Best Hundred Books,' &c. Most of it is useless and bewildering. The best advice I have ever seen in print about reading was by Sir Herbert Maxwell, and it appeared some years ago at the end of a *Nineteenth Century* article. It is as follows:

'If any young person of leisure were so much at a loss as to ask advice as to what he should read, mine should be exceedingly simple—*Read anything* bearing on a definite object. Let him take up any imaginable subject to which he feels attracted, be it the precession of the equinoxes or postage stamps, the Athenian drama or London street cries; let him follow it from book to book, and unconsciously his knowledge, not of that subject only, but of many subjects, will be increased, for the departments of the realm of[27] knowledge are divided by no *octroi*. He may abandon the first object of his pursuit for another; it does not matter, one subject leads to another; he will have acquired the habit of acquisition; he will have gained that conviction of the pricelessness of time which makes it intolerable for a man to lie abed of a morning.'

The art of reading is a thing to learn, and with it comes the equally valuable art of skipping.

Mr. Balfour's advice to readers is to learn the arts of skipping and skimming, and the late Philip Gilbert Hamerton said:—'The art of reading is to skip judiciously. The art is to skip all that does not concern us, whilst missing nothing that we really need. No external guidance can teach this; for nobody but ourselves can guess what the needs of our intellect may be.'

No one knows how to skim and skip who has not first well threshed out some subject for himself. No one can tear the heart out of a book who has not first been through the student period. Advice is poured forth in lengthy magazine articles, and lectures, but[28] as far as I know there is nothing which embodies such good sense on this subject, excepting Sir Herbert Maxwell's advice above, as a tiny pamphlet, about two inches square, written by Miss Lucy Soulsby, and sold for twopence. It is rather absurdly called *Things in Books Clothing!*

Below are printed only such passages, gathered from many sources, as I think are necessary to be known about the art of reading.

'It is true that the most absolute master of his own hours still needs thrift if he would turn them to account, and that too many *never* learn this thrift, whilst others learn it late..... Few intellectual men have the art of economising the hours of study. The very necessity which every one acknowledges of giving vast portions of life to attain proficiency in anything, makes us prodigal where we ought to be parsimonious, and careless where we have need of unceasing vigilance. The best time-savers are a love of soundness in all we learn or do, and a cheerful acceptance of inevitable limitations.'[10]

'In exchange for the varied pleasures of the[29] fashionable life, the intellectual life can offer you but one satisfaction, for all its promises are reducible simply to this, that you shall come at last, after infinite labour, into contact with some great *reality;* that you shall know and do in such sort that you will feel yourself on firm ground, and be recognised—probably not much applauded, but yet recognised—as a fellow-labourer by other knowers and doers. Before you come to this, most of your present accomplishments will be abandoned by yourself as unsatisfactory and insufficient, but one or two of them will be turned to better account, and will give you, after many years, a tranquil self-respect, and, what is still rarer and better, a very deep and earnest reverence for the greatness which is above you. Severed from the vanities of the illusory, you will live with the realities of knowledge as one who has quitted the painted scenery of the theatre to listen by the eternal ocean or gaze at the granite hills.'[11]

'Reading, with me, incites to reflection instantly. I cannot separate the origination of ideas from the reception of ideas. The consequence[30] is, as I read I always begin to think in various directions, and that makes my reading slow.'[12]

'When a particular object has to be attained, reading cannot be too special. There is an enormous waste of intelligence through a neglect of this fact, but otherwise reading should "come by nature." When I look through the list of The Best Hundred Books, I cannot help saying to myself, "Here are the most admirable and varied materials for the formation of a prig."'[13]

'Let us not be afraid of using a dictionary. *A* dictionary? A dozen; at all events, until Dr. Murray's huge undertaking is finished. And even then, for no one dictionary will help us through some authors—say, Chaucer, or Spenser, or Sir Thomas Browne. Let us use our full lexicon, and Latin dictionary, and French dictionary, and Anglo-Saxon dictionary, and etymological dictionary, and dictionaries of antiquity, and biography, and geography, and concordances, anything and everything that will throw light on the meanings and histories of words.'[14]

[31]

'To master a book, perhaps the best possible way is to write an essay in refutation of it. You may be bound few things will escape you then. The next best way may perhaps be to edit and annotate it for students, though, if some recent hebdomadal animadversions upon certain Oxford styles of annotation are well founded, this is questionable. The worst way, I should think, would be to review it for a newspaper.'[15]

'Reading, and much reading, is good. But the power of diversifying the matter infinitely in your own mind, and of applying it to every occasion that arises is far better.'[16]

'A person once told me that he never took up a book except with the view of making himself master of some subject which he was studying, and that while he was so engaged he made all his reading converge to that point. In this way he might read parts of many books, but not a single one from "end to end." This I take to be an excellent method of study, but one which implies the command of many books.'[17]

[32]

'Never read a book without pencil in hand. If you dislike disfiguring the margins and fly-leaves of your own books, borrow a friend's; but by all means use a pencil, if only to jot down the pages to be re-read. To transcribe striking, beautiful, or important passages is a tremendous aid to the memory; these will live for years, clear and vivid as day, when the book itself has become spectral and shadowy in the night of oblivion. A manuscript volume of such passages, well indexed, will become in time one of the most valuable books in one's library.'[18]

'No man, it appears to me, can tell another what he ought to read. A man's reading, to be of any value, must depend upon his power of association, and that again depends upon his tendencies, his capacities, his surroundings, and his opportunities.'[19]

I am fully convinced that the above passages condense all that is best worth knowing upon the 'Art of Reading.'

Next in importance is what to read. Be[33] very careful about reading books which are recommended, because they are books of the hour. Fools step in and say read this and that without thinking to put themselves in your place. Because a book suits one person, it is only a rare chance that it will suit a friend equally.

Before recommending a book to another with assurance, you must know the book well, and the friend to whom it is recommended you must know much better. Read the book which suggests something responsive and sympathetic. No one can tell you this as well as you can find it for yourself. Practice will teach you to choose a book, as practice has taught you to choose a friend. You will almost be able to choose it in the dark. There are affinities for books as for people, but this does not come at once.

The proper appreciation of the great books of the world is the reward of lifelong study. You must work up to them, and unconsciously you will become trained to find great qualities in what the world has decided is great. Novel reading is not a part of the intellectual life, it is a part of the fashionable life.[34]

Lamb says that Bridget Elia 'was tumbled early, by accident or design, into a spacious library of good old English reading, without much selection or prohibition, and browsed at will upon that fair and wholesome pasturage.' And he adds, 'Had I twenty girls they should be brought up exactly in this fashion.'

Ruskin says, 'there need be no choosing at all. Keep the modern magazine and novel out of your girl's way; turn her loose into the old library every wet day, and let her alone. She will find out what is good for her.'

Mr. Ruskin notwithstanding, there will ever be a large public who will read nothing unless it has a story in it.

Nearly all readers of books may be divided into two classes, those who read as students towards some definite end, and those who read for amusement. The latter class are greatly in the majority, and I have no hesitation in saying that a love of fiction will always predominate over a love of research, even in its light form. The student class, among whom are many critics, usually fail to understand the position of the fiction lovers, with the result that the fiction readers and fiction itself get a[35] great many jibes and taunts. To open this question would involve a long argument, and would bring about no good. All experience goes to prove that a very large section of the public, not being students, loves to read the books of the hour, and great pleasure may be got therefrom. The smaller section, trained to different habits, and regarding books in a more serious light, put their collection of books to different purposes, and, I know, get great pleasure therefrom. The two classes can run parallel together, and one class should not try to exterminate the other.[20] In country houses the books in billiard-rooms and in the bedrooms should appropriately be fiction. Not many guests at a house-party are in the frame of mind to take up serious books, nor are there the opportunities given for application which such would require. I think where the general house library is (as is very often the case) not a living room, there is then much more reason for separating fiction and light literature, and placing them in a very accessible position. It will often be found advisable, as fiction accumulates, to weed out and decide what volumes[36] shall be bound and what rejected or placed in the servants' library. Shelves should therefore be reserved for books which are thus going through a period of probation.[21]

A fiction library may be made very interesting if it is so arranged as to represent the history of France or of England, or any country. From the boundless stores of fiction writers—in fact, from Scott alone almost—a sequence of volumes may be arranged which, if read in proper order, would make a very excellent romance history. Almost every interesting episode of history has had its story woven into romance. Thus there are, I believe, about eighteen historical romances relating to the Monmouth rebellion alone.

'Much of love,' said Lord Bowen, 'has only been learned under the instruction of some woman who has herself only learned it from a book. Authoresses, indeed, have not unfrequently betrayed the key to some of their sex's secrets. Were it not for *Northanger Abbey* and Miss Austen, some of the old mysteries of girlish friendship would have remained untold, and we[37] should never have known or understood the curiosity which may lurk in a refined bosom at seventeen. Man would scarcely have guessed but for *Jane Eyre* the impression which can be made, it seems, upon a heart by a middle-aged gentleman with the manners of a bear and the composure of a prig. Furthermore, it is through women's novels that we have had brought home to us most adequately what women who have tasted it, or seen it, can best relate, the despicable egotism of a weak man. Anzoleto in *Consuelo*, Tito in *Romola*.'[22]

It is important for every one to fix upon a time for everyday study, and remember to read when you have a disposition so to do. Do not think that spare moments not spent in reading are lost. Some spare time must be kept for thinking. If you have 'nerves,' it is no good to read then; read when the mind is quiet and receptive. This will probably be when dressing in the morning, or at night before going to bed. Keep a small bookcase in your dressing-room; in so doing you will learn the art of going to bed well. Read at any time when curiosity is aroused as[38] to any person, place, or subject, and keep reference books at hand to answer questions intelligently. Napoleon read all the new novels in a travelling carriage, and pitched them out of the window as each was finished. Active minds, to read advantageously, should seek a quiet *sanctum* of their own.

A very admirable suggestion was made a short time since, I think by Dr. Ernest Hart, that it should be more a custom to have bookcases in bedrooms. Many persons, and, I believe, notably Mr. Gladstone, read before going to bed. I think all bedrooms should have a selection of favourite books, and I do not think that novels are nearly so suitable as books of short essays and sketches. Few people would sit up sufficiently long to read a novel through, and many would therefore not begin what they knew they would be unable to finish.

Common-place Books.

Very numerous methods have been suggested whereby memory may be assisted and the assimilation of our reading proceed without[39] indigestion. A reader is often pictured with note-book in hand, supposed to be memorising what he is reading. There is no doubt that note-books are very useful, but no note-book or commonplace-book should take the place of the natural memory—and every one has a good memory for something.

Thomas Fuller has wittily said, 'Adventure not all thy learning in one bottom, but divide it between thy memory and thy note-books..... A commonplace-book contains many notions in garrison, whence an owner may draw out an army into the field on competent warning.'

Every one has his and her own way of keeping a commonplace-book. Mr. Sala, I remember, once gave a minute account of his jottings in this way:[23] 'Todd's *Index Rerum* was,[40] in its day, very little else than an alphabeted book—a forerunner of what stationers now sell in various sizes called *Where is it?* The simplest form of commonplace-book is a[41] plain quarto MS. book ruled in an ordinary way, and in this entries may be made without being alphabeted. Do not write extracts or notes right across the line, but make your entries thus, having the keyword clear and easy to be seen:—

'PICUS DE MIRANDOLA.—His extraordinary gifts. His being sought
      after by women. Compare with H. T. Buckle. See also Hallam's
      Literary History, Part I. chap. iii.

In the matter of note-books, I am sure that it is best for every one to make notes in the way best suited to his convenience. Many, I think, find that taking notes while reading a book is an undesirable interruption. To such, it may be suggested to have slips of paper about half an inch wide, and four or five inches long, and insert these at the pages which contain anything notable. Then, when the book is finished, go through and transcribe or memorise such passages as are thus marked. I think it a great mistake to attempt too rigid a system in note-books, or too much red tape of any kind, because whenever this is done, the[42] time and thought, which should be given to the matter of the extract helping to fix it upon the memory, is given instead to the secondary matter of keeping your note-books very neat.

Reference Books.

I have been very often asked for a book which will 'tell one everything.' There is no such book, and there never could be such a book. Omniscience may be a foible of men, but it is not so of books. Knowledge, as Johnson said, is of two kinds, you may know a thing yourself, and you may know where to find it.[24] Now the amount which you may actually know yourself must, at its best, be limited, but what you may know of the sources of information may, with proper training, become almost boundless. And here come the value and use of reference books—the working of one[43] book in connexion with another—and applying your own intelligence to both. By this means we get as near to that omniscient volume which tells everything as ever we shall get, and although the single volume or work which tells everything does not exist, there is a vast number of reference books in existence, a knowledge and proper use of which is essential to every intelligent person. Necessary as I believe reference books to be, they can easily be made to be contributory to idleness, and too mechanical a use should not be made of them. Very admirable reference books come to us from America, where great industry is shown, and funds for publishing them never seem to be short. The French, too, are excellent at reference books, but the inferior way in which they are printed makes them tiresome to refer to. Larousse's *Grand Dictionnaire* is a miracle.

A good atlas is essential as a reference book, and maps of the locality where we live. A good map of old London is very useful in studying *Pepys' Diary* for instance. A good verbal dictionary is essential. Sometimes several should be in use: thus, Halliwell's[44] *Archaic Dictionary* and Nares' *Glossary* are useful in studying Shakespeare. Richardson's *Dictionary* embodies all the good points of Johnson's *Dictionary*, and is very excellent for quotations. Poetical *Concordances* and *Dictionaries of Quotations*, both prose and poetry, are useful, though very rarely does one find the quotation required in any professed book of quotations. A good *Biographical Dictionary* is a joy; such is Lippincott's, an American work. A good *Classical Dictionary* is also necessary, and may be supplemented by Smith's *Dictionary of Greek and Roman Biography*. It would be interesting to see how far it would be possible to collect an ideal reference library, and this, I think, has never been carefully done. It must be borne in mind that reference books are not all books arranged alphabetically (though the man who first wrote an alphabeted book should be Canonised). Reference books consist of such works as Rawlinson's Historical Works, Wilkinson's *History of the Ancient Egyptians*, and Fergusson's *History of Architecture*. All such books are reference books, and many thousands more. I think it will be found a good plan in the[45] library to keep reference books (viz., those which are likely to be in frequent use) in a separate case—perhaps a revolving case—and in no library should this section be neglected. Mr. Walter Wren, the well-known coach, once lectured on 'What is Education?' and in his lecture he made the following remarks:—

'I think the first thing that made me a teacher was my noticing, when a boy, how men and women read books and papers, and knew no more about them when they had read them than they did before..... Lots of people seem to know nothing, and to want to know nothing; at any rate, they never show any wish to learn anything. I was once in a room where not one person could say where Droitwich was; once, at a dinner of fourteen, where only one besides myself knew in what county Salisbury was. I have asked, I believe, over a hundred times where Stilton is, and have been told twice—this when Stilton cheese was handed. I mention this to show the peculiar conservative mental apathy of Englishmen.'

'A reader should be familiar with the best method by which the original investigation of[46] any topic may be carried on. When he has found it, he appreciates, perhaps for the first time, for what purpose books are for, and how to use them..... No person has any claim to be a scholar until he can conduct such an original investigation with ease and pleasure.' The foregoing was the advice of a well-known American librarian.

Boudoir Libraries.

Women have their own way of loving books. They are very rarely students, and more rarely still do they amass really great libraries, though many of the famous women of history have done so. Yet a woman likes to have her own books, and she likes, too, to have them separate from her husband's or her brothers', or the general family collection. Most women like tiny editions fitted into tiny cases.[25] Colour is much[47] more to a woman than to a man, and in the binding of her books she will very often be very happily inspired. I think that it is in De Maistre's *Journey Round my Room* that he says, 'It is certain that colours exercise an influence over us to the extent of rendering us gay or sad, according to their shades.' Charming tiny bookcases are now sold in various woods and in all sizes, and these have the advantage of being easily moved from place to place. A very pretty effect can be produced by a book-screen, but this, to be of service for taking books, must be placed in a room larger than most boudoirs. In choosing bindings for small books do not be surprised if, when bound, your books are not as flexible[48] as they should be. The easy opening of a book, and this particularly applies to small books, depends very much upon the thickness of the paper used, and small books printed on thick paper will never open well. Much blame is often heaped upon binders in this direction which is by no means their fault. Roan, parchment, vellum, morocco, and buckram are all suitable for boudoir bindings. Very pretty effects are produced by binding a series of small books in vellum with green lettering-pieces, and green edges instead of gilded edges. White backs, with pink or blue lettering-pieces, are also very dainty; and a pretty effect of another kind is produced by dark brown polished calf, with round backs, raised bands, and yellow edges.

Reference books, such as verbal dictionaries, dictionaries of quotations, a classical dictionary, an atlas, or a biographical dictionary, should always be to hand; and even when these are in the large library, duplicates should be kept in the boudoir.

In a very charming book, already referred to, called *The Story of my House*, there is certain practical advice which seems to be the[49] result of much experience and excellent taste on the part of the writer.

'With regard to the bookcases themselves, their height should depend upon that of the ceilings, and the number of one's volumes. For classification and reference it is more convenient to have numerous small cases of similar or nearly similar size, and the same general style of construction, than a few large cases in which everything is engulphed. With small or medium-sized receptacles, each one may contain volumes relating to certain departments or different languages, as the case may be; by this means a volume and its kindred may be readily found.'

'The style and colour of the bindings, also, may subserve a similar purpose; as, for instance, the poets in yellow or orange, books on nature in olive, the philosophers in blue, the French classics in red, &c. Unless methodically arranged, even with a very small library, a volume is often difficult to turn to when desired for immediate consultation, requiring tedious search, especially if the volumes are arranged upon the shelves with respect to size and outward symmetry. This may be[50] avoided by the use of small bookcases and a definite style of binding.'

I think here that the boudoir library should have its own catalogue, and every bookshelf marked or numbered. Every boudoir library should have a catalogue.

'In a room ten and a half to eleven feet high, five feet is a desirable height for the bookcases. Besides the drawers at the base, this will afford space for four rows of books, to include octavos, duodecimos, and smaller volumes. The shelves should, of course, be shifting. . . . . By leaving the top of the bookcase twelve to thirteen inches wide, ample space will be allowed for additional small books, porcelain, and *bric-à-brac*. It must be borne in mind that tall bookcases, in addition to the inaccessibility of the volumes in the upper shelves, have little, if any, space for pictures on the walls above them.'

It may be appropriate here to remind readers of an essay in Addison's *Spectator* upon my Lady's Library.

'Some months ago, my Friend, Sir Roger, being in the Country, enclosed a Letter to me, directed to a certain Lady, whom I shall[51] here call by the name of *Leonora*, and as it contained Matters of Consequence, desired me to deliver it to her with my own Hand. Accordingly, I waited upon her Ladyship early in the Morning, and was desired by her Woman to walk into her Lady's Library till such time as she was in Readiness to receive me. The very Sound of a *Lady's Library* gave me a great Curiosity to see it; and as it was some time before the Lady came to me, I had an Opportunity of turning over a great many of her Books, which were ranged together in very beautiful Order. At the end of the *Folios* (which were finely bound and gilt) were great Jars of *China*, placed one above another in a very noble piece of Architecture. The *Quartos* were separated from the *Octavos* by a Pile of smaller Vessels, which rose in a delightful Pyramid. The *Octavos* were bounded by Tea Dishes of all Shapes, Colours, and Sizes, which were so disposed on a wooden Frame that they looked like one continued Pillar indented with the finest Strokes of Sculpture, and stained with the greatest Variety of Dyes. That Part of the Library which was designed for the Reception of Plays and Pamphlets and other[52] loose Papers, was enclosed in a kind of Square, consisting of one of the prettiest Grotesque Works that ever I saw, and made up of Scaramouches, Lions, Monkies, Mandarines, Trees, Shells, and a thousand other odd Figures in *China* Ware. In the midst of the Room was a little Japan Table, with a Quire of gilt Paper upon it, and on the Paper a Silver Snuff-box, made in the Shape of a little Book. I found there were several other Counterfeit Books upon the upper Shelves, which were carved in Wood, and served only to fill up the Number, like Fagots in the muster of a Regiment. I was wonderfully pleased with such a mixt kind of Furniture, as seemed very suitable both to the Lady and the Scholar, and did not know at first whether I should fancy myself in a Grotto, or in a Library.'

Bookbinding.

As far as I am aware there are only four bookbinders in London who may be trusted not to mutilate a book, and there are only two who have any sense of design and harmony of colour. In sending a book to be[53] bound, if you value the book, you cannot be too careful or minute in giving instructions as to your wishes.

I think the best way to assist by advice is to picture a number of everyday instances of people requiring books to be bound, and to take such familiar cases instancing well-known books and show how each case can best be dealt with.

First of all, the right leather to use for binding is morocco. This is best; more durable, and a better choice of colour is given you. Half-morocco is good, but see that you get a good wide strip of morocco, and that it is not all cloth sides with a very narrow spine of leather. Valuable books should never be cut down. In many cases the top edges may be gilded which is a preservative from dust, but there are many other cases where instructions should be given to 'gild on the rough,' the three other sides should be left alone.

I will first take the case of the 'Cambridge' *Shakespeare*, the hand-made paper edition, already spoken of, where each play has been issued in a separate volume, and in all forty thin[54] volumes. Now the first question to settle is: Shall I have each of the forty volumes bound separately, or shall I bind the forty in twenty double volumes? or another question may arise in your mind, Shall I keep the book in its neat linen cover as published, and get another small paper copy, and bind that instead? Such questions must be settled—each one for himself. All I will say now is that the large paper forty volume edition when bound in twenty double volumes makes a very ideal copy of a great English classic; so, presuming that it is to be bound, you must choose the style of binding. It should rest between half-morocco and whole morocco, the latter costing about double the former. I think half-morocco is right for the book in most cases, whole morocco being unnecessarily expensive. Then comes colour, which must largely be referred to your own taste—olive-green, brown, dark red, and light apple green, would all be appropriate colours to choose from. The binder should have a book of colours and shades ready for you to select one from. Be sure and see that you have a coarse-grained levant morocco, which is much handsomer than the less good[55] hard fine-grained morocco; of course it should be a polished or crushed levant binding, though when you see the pattern piece of leather it will be rough and unpolished. At any rate select a colour which, when polished, will work '*clean.*' Do not select anything *very light* in morocco, it will probably not work 'clean,' but come out spotted even when new.

You will now select 'end papers.' These, I am sorry to say, are mostly very ugly, though there have recently been made some beautiful cloudy coloured papers, which now and then, and apparently by accident, are very beautiful, and they are also rather expensive. Some of the Japanese papers have pretty and very unobtrusive marblings worked upon them, and occasionally, too, a brocade paper looks well; but for a classic, the plainer the better, and very often a monotint end paper, or even a plain white, looks exceedingly well. In the matter of end and side papers, it is as well to know that these can very easily be altered even after the book is finished. The revival of flat backs has been the cause of some disputing. I think myself that the pleasure with which the trained eye[56] regards the flat back is sufficient excuse for it. As far as technique goes, the flat back is, I believe, just as lasting and as flexible as the round. Much must however be determined by the size and shape of the book as to whether a flat back is adopted or not. The *Shakespeare* which is now under consideration, when *bound in double volumes*, would, I think, look well with a flat back, and with flat raised bands between the panels; whereas, when bound in forty single volumes, it would be better to have a round back.

As to decoration and finish, the most lamentable errors of taste are often committed. Over-adornment is a curse. A person sees an attractive pattern lying in a shop, and wants all his or her books bound like it, without for a moment considering the anachronisms and impossible combinations that will thereby be perpetrated. It is the same with clothes. A man sees another man with a fine coat, and he straightway thinks he, too, will have a coat of that same make and pattern. Never does it occur to him to gauge the stature or character of the man who was first wearing the coat. There is yet a good deal of the monkey and[57] the ape left in us. We seem to do our best to stifle our individuality, and reduce our souls to one sad dead level of accursed and wicked imitation. Some day we shall have our eyes opened, and then see that a man may break the whole of the Ten Commandments at once, and yet he shall be saved if he be not vulgar, and it is both senseless and vulgar to copy old bindings on to modern books. The only decoration which the copy of Shakespeare could require is a gilt line, or double gilt lines, round the panels of the back. The full gilt back is fortunately becoming extinct. It may well die.

Decoration of books should only be carried out when we are sure we have an appropriate design, and when we are sure that the book is worth it.

There are now some other details to be looked after. I refuse to class them as minor details, because towards the making of the perfect book everything right is *essential*.

(1) The *Shakespeare*, being a book printed on paper of good quality, should have the top edge gilt, but the other sides should be left untouched or very slightly trimmed. (2) There should be one or two markers in each volume,[58] and the colour of these markers should harmonise with the colour of the binding. (3) The lettering should be chosen yourself. There should be a principal title *stamped boldly and deeply*, and subordinate lettering stamped lower down and in smaller type. Thus SHAKESPEARE'S WORKS or SHAKESPEARE merely in the top panel, with the editor's name underneath, and then below should be lettered the plays contained in each volume, and below that, at the foot, the date of publication. (4) Three weeks to a month at least should be allowed for the binding of such a work. (5) A folded copy in quires of a book is always preferable to a cloth-bound copy. (6) If a binder should ever suggest either a padded binding, a russia leather binding, or a tree calf binding, you may instantly leave his premises, for he cannot understand his business.

It will be understood that the rules which apply to the binding of this Shakespeare equally apply to most other books. I propose, however, to take such instances as I think present difficulties not already met, and see how they can be overcome.

A second instance shall be the new edition[59] of *Pepys' Diary*. The fact that this, and many other books, are published volume by volume makes it somewhat difficult to know whether to bind them at once or not to do so. In the case of the new edition of *Pepys' Diary*, as neither the binding of the large or small paper is unsightly, it should be left until complete, one good reason for this being that, if it be bound volume by volume as published, the binder will require a pattern volume each time, and your pattern volume will be lying about his workshop each time a volume is published. To register a pattern is by no means advisable in the case of a really well-bound series of books. It may do well enough for scientific and other journals, when great nicety of detail is not so much required. In the case of well-bound volumes, a pattern should accompany the order. A book like *Murray's Dictionary*, volumes of which are slow in completing themselves, the parts of the volumes, current and incomplete, should either be tied up in paper, and kept together, or they should be placed between two pieces of millboard on the shelf where they will finally be placed.

A third instance shall be an old book which[60] requires repairing or restoring. We will suppose that it is an old copy of *Clarissa Harlowe*, which you have picked up on a country book-stall. Now the binding is probably very much broken, and, being very dry, is getting rapidly worse. It is time, therefore, that it went into hospital, and at the bookbinder's hospital very clever operations are performed. To restore a binding, paste is rubbed over the leather, and, after it is dry, it is washed over with a thin solution of glue size. Again, when dry, the volume is varnished and afterwards rubbed over with a cloth upon which a few drops of sweet oil have been dropped. Here is one operation just in outline. There are very many others, which I can only refer to. If there are ink marks on any of the volumes of your *Clarissa*, which you wish removed, this can probably be done so that no trace is left. Similarly many grease-spots can be effectually removed. If a page is torn, it can be repaired, or if a piece of it is missing, it can be facsimiled, and the whole of the inside of the volume can be washed throughout. Never destroy an old binding if you can help it, and never obliterate marks of ownership, for it is[61] interesting to trace the owners of a book. If a bookplate is in your *Clarissa*, and you wish your own to appear, transplant the former one to the end cover, and put your own in the front if you wish. Never have such a book as we are now discussing cut down. A book has recently been written and published by Mr. C. G. Leland on *Mending and Repairing*, in which the author recommends the amateur to repair his own books. I believe Mr. Leland is an expert hand at many arts and crafts, but I do not think that every amateur should attempt experiments in repairing his own books unless he means to give a great deal of time to it, which very few would, I think, care to do.

The following remarks, taken from a review, I think by Mr. A. Lang, are valuable:—'The binder is often very mischievous. He not only "cuts down" books, impairing their shapeliness and ruining them for sale, nay, even cutting off lines, but he is apt to lose fly-leaves, with imprints, and rare autographs. What he rejects may have a merely fanciful or sentimental interest, still that interest can be expressed in terms of currency. An eighth of an inch in margin may represent a large[62] sum of money, and it is just as easy not to cut down the volume. Old bookplates ought to be kept, on new bindings of old books. They are the pedigree of a volume. The ancient covers, if discarded, should be examined. They are often packed with fragments of old manuscripts, deeds, woodcuts, or engravings. The ages have handed books on to us; it is our duty to hand them on to coming generations, clean, sound, uninjured.'

The fourth case shall be paper-bound novels, English and French editions, and Tauchnitz copies. I have no hesitation in saying that the best material is Buckram. It has the merit of being good—that is to say, durable, cheap, artistic, and not harsh to handle, as many linens are. There are some half-a-dozen good colours in Buckram, and these, when relieved by lettering-pieces of some contrasting colour, can be made most decorative and economical. I believe buckram is in every way a most excellent material for binding, and for students who buy and use German and French textbooks published in paper, this material is excellent for their libraries as well.

Here may be added a few words as to Pamphlets[63] and Magazines. It has been recommended that Pamphlets be kept in boxes, which may be placed upon the shelves as books, but this will not be found either convenient or secure. The best way is to bind Pamphlets in volumes according to size, or if *very* numerous, according to date or subject, and let them each be entered separately in the catalogue. In the cataloguing of private libraries it is sometimes thought that certain sections, such as pamphlets and magazines, are not worth entering, but the only safe rule is that, if it is worth keeping, it is worth cataloguing. Single pamphlets should be bound in limp roan, and volumes of pamphlets in buckram or half-calf, with full lettering on the back.

Magazines, when they are kept complete, should, of course, be bound up in their volumes, either yearly or half-yearly; but it often happens that a magazine is bought for a single article, and many of these accumulating, it is quite easy for such articles as are of special interest to be taken from the remainder, and treated as pamphlets. In the case of magazines and scientific periodicals of importance, it is well to keep the covers and bind them at the end of[64] each volume. Music should be bound in limp roan in preference to limp calf, because the latter would sooner show scratches and marks, particularly as a large surface is exposed.

If you want your pamphlets and novels to look nice, beware of your binder using what he calls his odd pieces, generally monsters of ugliness.

Family papers, autograph letters, and MS. matter of all kinds should be placed in the hands of an expert, with instructions to calendar them, viz., catalogue them, giving a *précis* of the contents of each one. They should then be mounted and bound up in volumes, with abstract of contents in front of the volume. It will be well to consider the advisability of having typed copies made of the whole wherever unpublished records exist.

Much, very much, more might be written about practical details in bookbinding, but nothing is so valuable as experience, and a few mistakes will be the best teacher. Remember that morocco is the best material, whether it be half or whole morocco, pigskin is second, calf is third, vellum is fourth, roan is fifth, buckram is sixth, though it may frequently take the place of calf.

[65]

Book Hobbies.

It has been remarked that only an auctioneer admires all schools of literature. I think it is certain that the way to get most enjoyment from books is to specialise a little. Mr. Pepys, it will be remembered, collected Black Letter Ballads, Penny Merriments, Penny Witticisms, Penny Compliments, and Penny Godlinesses, and what Pepys paid a penny for are now worth much gold. Lord Crawford is, I believe, one of the most enthusiastic among present day collectors, and I am told that he spends many hours in arranging and cataloguing his extensive and curious collection. As far as I can gather from the printed catalogues which have been issued of Lord Crawford's library, he is rivalling Pepys in his collection of ballads. Other subjects which he has taken up are proclamations and Papal bulls. I cannot omit saying that if Lord Crawford's example were followed by a few more rich men, they would find therein very amusing hobbies. The catalogues of the Ballads and the Proclamations in the Library at Haigh Hall have been compiled by Lord[66] Crawford's own hand, and there are no better catalogues of a private collection in existence. The late Lord Braybrooke collected County histories, and got together a most valuable and interesting collection. But, judging from his own account of his collection,[26] it was too general to be very interesting. There is hardly a more useful or profitable book hobby than the collecting of Topographical books, but each one should confine himself to one County, or at most two, and even with discrimination in buying, a single County collection soon becomes extensive. What should be aimed at in such a collection is the putting together whatever will illustrate the archæology, general history, folk lore, dialect, and natural history, of a district or County, and wherever there is a Church and a Manor, there is a history. Each parish history is the unit of the history of the nation, and any one investigating the parochial history of a single parish will find much national history written in between the lines. With regard to topographical and genealogical books, I may say that the prices of these are rapidly rising, and will continue to[67] rise, owing largely to the increasing competition in America for these books.

Sir Walter Gilbey has, it is well known, a fine collection of sporting books. There is no sport but what has its literature, and if there is one subject more than another, upon which the English mind is unchanging, it is sport, and this being so, sporting books will always offer a fine field for collectors. As the coaching age recedes farther back, so it will be found that an increasing number of men will want to read about what they no longer can hear *viva voce*. All out-door subjects are good hobbies. Flower culture and the laying out of grounds, birds and natural history generally are good subjects, but it must be understood that no one can find another a subject, one can only *suggest*, and that is all I propose to do here. Books offer a very endless variety of hobbies. So I have merely named one or two highways, and there is an endless maze of bypaths which offer delightful hunting grounds. Dr. Johnson, it may be remembered, expressed a very sound commonsense view of this matter to Boswell:

'When I mentioned that I had seen in the King's Library fifty-three editions of my[68] favourite *Thomas à Kempis* .... in eight languages .... Johnson said he thought it unnecessary to collect many editions of a book which were all the same except as to paper and print. He would have the original, and all the translations, and all editions having variations in the text. He approved of the famous collection of the editions of Horace by Douglas, and, he added, "Every man should try to collect one book in that manner. . . . ."'

Old Country Libraries.

The library of Chaucer's Clerk of Oxenford, which represented about the maximum that an ordinary student would possess, consisted of

'A twenty bokes, clothed in black and red,
Of Aristotle and his philosophie,'

and these he kept 'at his beddes hed.'

Dr. Jessopp, in one of his learned papers,[27] has pointed out that in the thirteenth century the number of books in the world was, to say the least, small. A library of five hundred volumes would, in those days, have been considered[69] an important collection, and after making all due allowances for ridiculous exaggerations, which have been made by ill-informed writers on the subject, it may safely be said that nobody in the thirteenth century—at any rate in England—would have erected a large and lofty building as a receptacle for books, simply because nobody could have contemplated the possibility of filling it. Here and there amongst the larger and more important monasteries there were undoubtedly collections of books, the custody of which was entrusted to an accredited officer, but the time had not yet come for making libraries well stored with such priceless treasures as Leland, the antiquary, saw at Glastonbury, just before that magnificent foundation was given as a prey to the spoilers. A library, in any such sense as we now understand the term, was not only no essential part of a monastery in those days, but it may almost be said to have been a rarity.

In the twelfth and thirteenth centuries we rarely meet with any indications of a literary taste among the laity; the books they purchased were more for ornament than use.[70] But in the fifteenth century we find books mentioned in a manner which would seem to indicate that the laity were enabled to use them with pleasure. In 1395, Alice, Lady West, left to Joan, her son's wife, 'all her books of Latin, English, and French;' and from the memoranda of Sir John Howard, we learn that that worthy knight could read at his leisure 'an Englyshe boke, callyd *Dives et Pauper*,' for which, and 'a Frenshe boke,' in 1464, he paid thirteen shillings and fourpence. The library of this member of the Howard family was sufficiently extensive to enable him to select therefrom, on the occasion of his going to Scotland, thirteen volumes for his solace and amusement on the voyage.[28] In the Paston *Letters* will be found a catalogue of the library of one of the members of this fifteenth century family. In the monasteries books were, of course, used and treasured long before they became part of the household goods of rich laymen. The catalogue of the House of the White Canons, at Titchfield, in Hampshire, dated 1400, shows that the books were kept in a small room on[71] shelves, and set against the walls. A closet of this kind was evidently not a working place, but simply a place of storage. By the beginning of the fifteenth century, the larger monasteries had accumulated many hundred volumes, and it began to be customary to provide for the collections separate quarters, rooms constructed for the purpose. The presses in the cloisters were still utilised for books in daily reference.[29] Duke Humphrey was a great book collector and patron of letters, and presented to the University of Oxford many of the illuminated treasures which he had collected. The magnificent collection of Charles V. of France, also a great bibliomaniac, was brought by the Duke of Bedford into England. This library contained 853 volumes of great splendour, and the introduction of these books into England stimulated a spirit of inquiry among the more wealthy laymen. Guy Beauchamp, Earl of Warwick, collected a very fine library of early romances, which about 1359, he left to the monks of Bordesley Abbey, in Worcestershire. A list of this library will[72] be found in Todd's *Illustrations of Gower and Chaucer.*

Mr. J. W. Clark has, with quite wonderful learning, drawn a picture of student-life of the past with such graphic vigour that we can almost reinstate Colet, Casaubon, and Erasmus, and picture them exactly as they worked among their books. In Macaulay's chapter upon *The State of England in 1685*, are given numerous facts about the difficulty the clergy had in getting books, and the little desire there was among the squires to possess libraries. Few knights of the shire had libraries so good as may now perpetually be found in a servants' hall, or in the back parlour of a small shopkeeper. An esquire passed among his neighbours for a great scholar if *Hudibras* and *Baker's Chronicle*, *Tarleton's Jests*, and the *Seven Champions of Christendom*, lay in his hall window among the fishing rods and fowling pieces. No circulating library, no book society, then existed, even in the capital; but in the capital those students who could not afford to purchase largely had a resource. The shops of the great booksellers, near St. Paul's Churchyard, were[73] crowded every day and all day long with readers. In the country there was no such accommodation, and every man was under the necessity of buying whatever he wished to read. Macaulay further points out that Cotton seems, from his *Angler*, to have found room for his whole library in his hall window; and Cotton was a man of letters. In the *Life of Dr. John North* there is an account of that delightful person's dealings with Mr. Robert Scott, of Little Britain, a very famous bookseller in the seventeenth century.

Dr. John North is really a fascinating personality.[30] His soul was 'never so staked down as in an old bookseller's shop, for, having taken orders, he was restless till he had compassed some of that sort of furniture as he thought necessary for his profession.

'I have borne him company,' says his biographer, 'at shops for hours together, and, minding him of the time, he hath made a dozen proffers before he would quit. By this care and industry he made himself master of a very considerable library, wherein the choicest collection was Greek.'

[74]

Pepys wished that his name should go down to posterity as a man fond of books. The arrangements for the settlement of his library after death prove this. The numerous references throughout the *Diary* show that he had a passion for collecting, and showed good judgment in what he got together. Pepys, like Dr. John North, dealt of Robert Scott, who, when sending his distinguished customer four scarce books, the total cost of which was only 1*l*. 14*s*., writes, 'Without flattery I love to find a rare book for you.'[75][31]

R. SCOTT, the bookseller, to Mr. PEPYS.

'*June 30th, 1688.*

'SIR,—Having at length procured Campion, Hanmer, & Spencer's Hist. of Ireland, fol. (which I think, you formerly desired) I here[76] send itt you, with 2 very scarce bookes besides, viz. Pricaei Defensio Hist. Britt. 4to, and old Harding's Chronicle, as alsoe the Old Ship of Fooles, in old verse, by Alex. Berkley, priest;[77] which last, though nott scarce, yett soe very fayre and perfect, that seldome comes such another; the Priceus you will find deare, yett I never sold it under 10*s*., and att this tyme you can have it of a person of quality; butt I love to find a rare book for you, and hope shortly to procure for you a perfect Hall's Chronicle.

'I am, Sir,
'Your Servant to command,
'ROBERT SCOTT.'

Campion, Hanmer, & Spencer fol.	0:12:0
Hardings Chronicle, 4to.	0: 6:0
Pricaei Defens. Hist. Britt.	0: 8:0
Shipp of Fooles, fol.	0: 8:0
	1:14:0

The contents of Pepys' famous collections of Manuscripts, Books and rare single-sheet literature are known more or less to students, and are found by them to be of the utmost value. It is amusing to notice how careful Pepys was not to admit into his library any 'risky' books. Little did he think that the[78] key to the diary would be one day discovered. When he bought in the Strand 'an idle, rogueish, French book, *L'Escholle des Filles*,' he resolved, as already stated, as soon as he had read it, to burn it, 'that it might not stand in the list of books, nor among them, to disgrace them, if it should be found.' He was equally solicitous about Rochester's *Poems*.

Pepys' books were numbered consecutively throughout the library, and therefore, when rearranged, they needed to be all renumbered. This was done by Pepys himself, his wife, and Deb Willett, who were busy until near midnight 'titleing' the books.

With so many references to Pepys and his book-collecting as we find in the *Diary*, it is puzzling to read, under date, October 5, 1665, after references to 'Sister Poll,' 'I abroad to the office, and thence to the Duke of Albemarle, all my way reading a book of Mr. Evelyn's translating and sending me as a present, about directions for gathering a library, *but the book is above my reach*.' Pepys, one would think, had by this time gone far enough in himself gathering a library to understand the little pamphlet by[79] Naudeus, librarian to Cardinal Mazarin, which Evelyn translated, and which was issued in 1661, and which is now very rare. There is a charming letter from Evelyn to Pepys, dated 12th August, 1689, giving very many interesting details of the private libraries of the seventeenth century, and which goes a very long way to modify Macaulay's rather overdrawn picture of the scarcity of books and private libraries in 1685. This letter of Evelyn's might be compared with Addison's picture of 'Tom Folio' in the *Tatler*.[36] Tom Folio stood for a great book collector, Thomas Rawlinson.

The eighteenth century produced a host of great book collectors. William Oldys, Humphrey Wanley, and Thomas Rawlinson just mentioned. These men were great experts, who infected with enthusiasm many great patrons of letters, such as Charles, Earl of Sunderland, the Earl of Pembroke, Lord Somers, Lord Oxford, Topham Beauclerk, Colonel Stanley, and George Earl Spencer, whose famous Library now at Manchester has been called the finest private[80] library in Europe. In his *Life of Sir Walter Scott*, Lockhart has inserted a visitor's impression of the library at Abbotsford. 'The visitor might ransack a library, unique, I suppose, in some of its collections, and in all departments interesting and characteristic of the founder. So many of the volumes were enriched with anecdotes or comments in his own hand, that to look over his books was, in some degree, conversing with him.' The catalogue of the Abbotsford library was printed by the Maitland Club in 1838, and is one of the best catalogues of a private collection ever printed.

Weeding Out.

It is necessary that a large country-house library should occasionally be weeded out and overhauled. The libraries which were formed in past generations cannot be expected to suit present-day requirements. In a great many country-house libraries there is little else than a great mass of turgid theology, but very often buried among these are really valuable[81] books. Upon the death of the head of a family, the library should be carefully gone over in order that the new owner may get an idea of the books—a collection which he may be excused from knowing much of as he did not collect it. The books should then be re-arranged to suit the views of those who are most likely to use them, and certain rejected volumes should be disposed of and others put in their places.

How much this is necessary might be illustrated by many anecdotes.

The Catalogue.

I have said, under the heading 'Classification,' that it is not advisable or necessary to attempt any rigid classification upon the shelves. One good reason for this is that by so doing you are trying to do what can so much better be done by a catalogue. No one who uses books very much but sooner or later becomes grateful for the existence of an alphabet and an arrangement by A B C. Carlyle once said, 'A library is not worth[82] anything without a catalogue; it is a Polyphemus without any eye in his head, and you must confront the difficulties, whatever they may be, of making proper catalogues.'

'The classification of Pepys' library was to be found in the catalogues, and as Pepys increased in substance he employed experts to do this work for him.'[37]

No catalogue is of any use unless you can tell from it (1) All that the library possesses of the known books of a known author at one view, as well as (2) All that it possesses, by whomsoever written, on a known and definite subject.

The old catalogues were mostly very bad. Old methods have now given way to newer and better bibliographical systems, and, to take the case of a large country house, where books are scattered about in many rooms, a catalogue is most essential. The catalogue should, in most cases, be in MS., and not typewritten. Such an arrangement admits of additions being made more easily. The printed catalogue is adopted where the library is of special value, or if it has any particular class of books predominating[83] to make it of use as a bibliography of a special subject. Lord Crawford's sectional catalogues of his library, already referred to, are the most valuable lists I know of for student purposes, but I believe very few people have ever seen them.

The catalogue of Lord Crawford's Proclamations, at Haigh Hall, is a marvel of industry and accuracy. Mr. Locker Lampson's Rowfant Library was catalogued, and the catalogue printed and sold, because it had special value as a collection of Elizabethan poetry. Mr. Edmund Gosse's Library catalogue was printed because it contained special collections of seventeenth-century literature. Whether the library be a student's library or a general library, a catalogue is essential. Gibbon had a catalogue of his books. I have seen so many amateur attempts at cataloguing private libraries that I am bound to say I do not think the plan of cataloguing one's own books in any way answers. Any catalogue may be better than no catalogue, but, if a catalogue is to be done, it is better by far to call in the assistance of some one whose work it is. It frequently happens that a[84] family inherits a large library, and the inheritors, not having formed the collection, naturally can know but little, if anything, of its contents. Now, in such a case, and in many other cases, the best plan is to have your books overhauled, sifted, certain volumes weeded out, if necessary, others rebound, and the whole remainder carefully catalogued and described, the cases being numbered and the shelves lettered.

Very often the owner of a library sets out to catalogue his or her own books, and makes the initial mistake of entering them one by one in a MS. volume already bound up. Such a plan must end in failure and disorder, because it is impossible by this means to get the titles strictly alphabetical. Others I have seen commence writing the titles from the backs of the books. Other difficulties which are encountered are with anonymous books, and with such authors as used pseudonyms, and, in some cases, many pseudonyms. Such was Henri Beyle, whose books bear various disguises, such as De Stendhal, Cotonet, Salviati, Viscontini, Birkbeck, Strombeck, César Alexandre Bombet.[85] The British Museum Library has ninety-one rules of cataloguing, forming, perhaps, the best cataloguing code in the world; but for private libraries such elaboration and detail is not necessary. The following are the main rules to be adopted in private libraries:—[38]

1. The catalogue should be arranged in one general alphabet, this being the most useful and the readiest form for reference. To render it, as nearly as possible, a correct representation of the contents of the library, each work has but one principal descriptive entry. The shelfmark is confined to this entry—duplicate shelfmark references, when the position of books is likely to be often altered, from the accession of additions to the library, &c., leading to frequent and unavoidable errors.

2. This entry is under the author's name when given on the title-page, or otherwise known, as being the only arrangement which allows one general rule to be followed throughout the catalogue.

3. Anonymous works, whose authors' names[86] are unknown, are placed under the subjects to which they relate.

4. Cross references are made:
from the subjects of biographies to the authors;
from the principal anonymous and pseudonymous works to the writer's real names where known;
from works included in, or noticed in the title-pages of other publications, to those publications.

5. To obviate the imperfections necessarily attendant on an alphabetical arrangement, and for the greater facility of reference, short classifications are introduced of the chief subjects on which the books in the library treat, referring to the names of the authors in the same general alphabet; thereby uniting the advantages of the alphabetical and classified systems, and acting in some measure as a key to the prevailing character of the library.

6. All authors' names are followed by full stops: any articles placed under a writer's name, of which he is not the author, but which are anonymous answers to, or criticisms on, his[87] works; anonymous memoirs placed under the subjects; or any entries whatever, in which the heading name prefixed is not that of the author, are distinguished by a line following the name.

7. The headings of the short classifications are distinguished by being doubly underlined with red ink. The name to be referred to is singly underlined, but when the reference is to another heading, and not to an author, it is doubly underlined.

In preparing titles for the catalogue (whether it be intended to transcribe or print them), it should be an imperative instruction that they be written on slips of paper (or on cards) of uniform size. It is also useful to include in them a word or two which may serve to identify the origin of the books—whether by purchase, by copyright, or by gift—and to indicate the date of their respective acquisition.

Classification of Books.

The classification of books, according to any set system, or according to subjects upon the shelves of a library, is not easy, and for many[88] reasons it is not worth attempting. Unless the library is a very large one, say, ten to twenty thousand volumes, with ample and adaptable shelving, it is not to be desired. The main difficulty in shelf classification lies in the fact that books on similar and kindred subjects are issued in all sizes. There are books on Furniture, for instance, in folio, in quarto, and in octavo. When shelf classification is imperative, the folios are all put together, the quartos together, and the octavos together. This is the nearest realisation of a shelf classification, and by this method the folios may be far separated from the quartos, and the quartos from the octavos. Moreover, if appearance count for anything, as indeed it should in the most modest library, it will be impossible to carry out any plan of shelf classification and preserve at the same time an appearance of method and fitness. In planning out how your books are to be placed, a great consideration is the placing of them, so that books likely to be frequently referred to shall be easy of access, and books less likely to be in request shall be housed higher up.[39] Reference[89] books should, as far as possible, be placed together, and all easy of access. The main divisions into which a private library classes itself are History and Biography, Fiction, Poetry and Drama, Theology, Travel, Art, Belles lettres; but there are so many considerations besides those of subject in any general classification which should determine the position of a volume that I must emphasise what has already been said about actual personal convenience being first studied, and the library as arranged on the shelves should be the result of personal convenience and graceful effect. This is more particularly necessary when a library is in course of expansion. The subjects which will expand quickest, and the space they will require, can never be accurately gauged, and frequent upheavals and readjustments will be necessary if any rigid plan is aimed at. I would suggest that a separate shelf—or, if necessary, a separate case—be reserved for unbound periodicals and for accessions, which are, as it were, *sub judice*. Often, too, a separate case is necessary for rare and handsome books, and a locked case for *facetiæ*. It is worth while to observe that Pepys found that the best way to[90] find his numerous books was to number them consecutively throughout the library.[40]

Numerous elaborate plans of book classification have been put forward, principally by Americans, but in no way are they adaptable to the requirements of private libraries, and I doubt very much the possibility of comprehending them in such a way as to apply them in an intelligible manner even to public libraries.

Mr. B. R. Wheatley, in an admirable paper[91] upon Library arrangement,[41] gives the following excellent practical advice:—

'If I had the planning of rooms for a private library, I should select as the best possible arrangement a suite of three rooms, or one long room or gallery divided by columns into three compartments, of which the centre should be the largest, with several small contiguous ante-rooms, the entrances to which, if so desired, might be concealed, for uniformity or completeness of appearance, by filling them with sham or dummy book-backs, the titles of which may be made an occasion for witticism or joking allusion to local and family history.

'A good library arrangement is not achieved at once, but is a slow growth through difficulties met and conquered. Some of the best portions of it will be those which have flashed across your mind when there seemed no pathway out of the thicket of difficulty in which you were struggling. The arrangement of books, where the shelves are not made to order to suit your plans, must naturally be of a progressive character in its development in your mind.

'In some old libraries, collected mostly in[92] the seventeenth and eighteenth centuries, there is such a preponderance of those portly tomes in folio in which our sturdy ancestors delighted, that they materially affect and disconcert our ordinary plans. I have known an instance in which the library shelves projected slightly in their upper part, and, there thus being an appropriate depth, I arranged on these shelves two long parallel rows, completely round the room, of these noble volumes of our old divines, State papers, Statutes, Treaties, Trials, and our County histories; and the effect in strength and power (as Ruskin might have said) of these long lines of large stout books of nearly equal height and size was really magnificent. Sometimes you meet with such a valuable and massive body of topography as will not allow of its cavalierly being made a subsidiary section of the class of history, and the form and weighty character of the folios suggest that some deep and separate bookcases should be chosen in which it may assume the important individuality that it deserves.

'Folios of a modern date, being of very unequal sizes, would have a raggedness of outline which would be less observed nearer[93] to the ground than in the elevated position just referred to. As a general rule, a row of folios on the lowest shelf will be succeeded by one of quartos, and then above the ledge the octavos and duodecimos will be placed, but they should not ascend in too rigid a law of gradual decrease. Rows of small books at the top of a bookcase look as petty to the mind as to the eyes, and, indeed, are in general more appropriately placed in dwarf bookcases specially fitted for their reception.

'For small libraries, not exceeding 3000 to 4000 volumes, the letters of the alphabet may be used for the cases, and small figures for the shelves, on the principle of the greater including the less, the letters having a more important appearance. But in larger libraries, where there is a chance of the alphabet being doubled or trebled, one regular series of large numbers for the cases, with small letters for the shelves, is to be preferred.'

Books should be marked in pencil, with a shelf letter and a case number.

Long sets of books need be numbered in the first volume only.[94]

In the case of collections of pamphlets each item ought to be separately catalogued.

The catalogue should complement the arrangement on the shelves, and not be tautological.

Tables of contents of collected editions given in catalogue.

A synoptical table of contents should be prefixed to the catalogue.

For those who desire a rough outline of headings into which a library usually classifies itself, I will name one. The briefest is as follows:—(1) Theology, (2) Philosophy and Science, (3) Art, (4) Political Economy, (5) Law, (6) History and Literature.

Bookcases.

The chief faults of bookcases arise from their being designed and made by men who have never used a book. A first requisite in bookcases is simplicity, bearing in mind that the books are the ornament and not the bookcases. The cabinet-maker, among other things, is too fond of embellishments, and[95] sacrifices space to what seem odd angularities and irregularities.

No bookcase should be above eight and a half feet in height. No ladder should be necessary to get at books. If books are 'skied' up to the ceiling they must suffer from the heated air. It is heat, not gas merely, which damages books.

A room may be made to look very beautiful by being surrounded with fumed oak bookcases, eight feet high. The shelves should be made movable with Tonks' patent.[42] Mr.[96] Gladstone[43] speaks of the looseness and the tightness of movable shelves, the weary arms, the aching fingers, and the broken finger-nails. This can be avoided by the use of the patent here named. The bottom cases should be deeper and wider, to take quartos and folios, but there should always be an extra shelf for turning a folio section into an octavo section. Nineteen-twentieths of the books in circulation are octavos and smaller volumes. On each side of the fireplace there should be an arm projecting about four feet and a half. The inner side of this should have a comfortable reading-seat, and on the outer side, farthest from the fire, there may be shelves for books. If the structural arrangements of the room admit of[97] these projecting arms being placed, without sacrifice of comfort, at a greater distance from the fireplace, the books may be placed on the upper part of the inner side as well, the lower part being used as a lounge.

It must be remembered that heat and excessive dryness are fatal to good bindings and, indeed, to all parts of a book, and therefore no bookcase should approach too near a fireplace, nor should bookcases be placed backing upon hot-water pipes. The shelves should be edged with leather and such leather must *not* be stiffened by cardboard or brown paper—simply leather, and there should be a roller shutter of silk to draw down in front of the books during absence from home. The cases[44] should everywhere be perfectly flush, without any sort of protruding ornament. It will be found a great advantage to make the framework of the various cases of equal dimensions, so that the shelves can be made transferable. In estimating the extent of shelving which it may be necessary to provide, we may calculate that in an ordinary library a space[98] two feet high and two feet wide will, on an average, contain about thirty-five volumes, and it may be estimated roughly that every thousand volumes in a library will require about a hundred square feet of shelving.

If fixed shelves are made, the usual height will be—[45]

For folios	18 to 21 inches.
" quartos	12 " 15 "
" octavos	10 "
" smaller sizes	7 "

[99]

These spaces will allow ample room for the average sizes. The 'Atlas' folios and 'Elephant' folios are best accommodated in single shelves, in which they may be flat, or on trays or table cases.[46] Bear in mind always to allow sufficient space for expansion. Nothing causes more disorder than insufficient shelf accommodation. All cases should be numbered and lettered, that is, each section should have a number, and each shelf a letter. For the accommodation of expensive bindings or rare books and MSS., a special case may sometimes be required. Very beautiful specimens of such may be seen sketched in the books of Chippendale, Sheraton, and Heppelwhite, but it is in all cases better to avoid glass fronts and adopt ornamental brass wire work if any special protection be needed.

The late Mr. Blades, a great expert in this matter, said, 'It is a mistake to imagine that keeping the best-bound volumes in a glass-doored bookcase is a preservative. The damp air will certainly penetrate, and as the absence of ventilation will assist formation of mould, the books will be worse off than if they had been[100] placed in open shelves. If securing be desirable, by all means abolish the glass and place ornamental brass wire work in its stead.'[47]

'It is more important to see that the shelves intended for choice and richly bound books should be covered with leather, and expressly such as are intended for books of large sizes. In the case of books of special value, the leather should be well padded, should be of the best quality, and should have a polished surface.'[48]

In the *Nineteenth Century* for March, 1890, already quoted from, Mr. Gladstone wrote upon 'Books, and the Housing of them.' This paper showed a sound grasp of the subject and showed Mr. Gladstone in a new and very interesting light. Appended are some extracts from this paper, all of which I think experts would agree to, *except the fixed shelves*, and here, I think, any one who has handled books very much will be at issue with Mr. Gladstone. He himself says:—'I have recommended that, as a rule, the shelves be fixed, and have given reasons for the adoption[101] of such a rule. I do not know whether it will receive the sanction of authorities, and I make two admissions. First, it requires that each person owning and arranging a library should have a pretty accurate general knowledge of the size of his books. Secondly, it may be expedient to introduce here and there, by way of exception, a single movable shelf.'

Now, a man must be able not only to gauge very accurately the limits of his library and the various sizes of books, but he must be able to look into the future if he would safely embark on fixed shelves. And this is wholly impossible. Fixed shelves should only be adopted where cost has to be reduced to a minimum, but in the majority of instances movable shelves will be found preferable. The paragraphs which deal with bookcases in Mr. Gladstone's article may here be given:—

'The question of economy, for those who from necessity or choice consider it at all, is a very serious one. It has been a fashion to make bookcases ornamental. Now, books want for and in themselves no ornament at all. . . The man who looks for society in his books will readily perceive that, in proportion as the[102] face of his bookcase is occupied by ornament, he loses that society; and conversely, the more that face approximates to a sheet of book-backs, the more of that society he will enjoy. And so it is that three great advantages come hand in hand, and, as will be seen, reach their maximum together: the sociability of books, minimum cost in providing for them, and ease of access to them.

'In order to attain these advantages, two conditions are fundamental. First, the shelves must, as a rule, be fixed; secondly, the cases, or a large part of them, should have their side against a wall, and thus, projecting into the room for a convenient distance, they should be of twice the depth needed for a single line of books, and should hold two lines, one facing each way. Twelve inches is a fair and liberal depth for two rows of octavos. The books are thus thrown into stalls, but stalls after the manner of a stable. . . . This method of dividing the longitudinal space by projections at right angles to it, if not very frequently used, has long been known. A great example of it is to be found at Trinity College, Cambridge, and is the work of Sir Christopher Wren. He[103] has kept these cases down to a very moderate height; for he doubtless took into account that great heights require long ladders, and that the fetching and use of these greatly add to the time consumed in getting or replacing a book.'

It must here be added that Mr. Gladstone's plan is much more fitted for a large public library than for the library of a private person, for whom he is prescribing. Though the library in the form of an annexe[49] is in many ways an ideal form for housing a large library, yet these are hardly likely to be in the majority, and most people find that they have to house their books in a circumscribed space, with no room for such bays and projections as he suggests except perhaps one by the fireplace.

Miscellaneous Appliances.

Whether the library be considered as a workshop or a morning-room, there are certain necessary appliances, which will contribute a great deal to comfort, and the proper preservation of books. Thus, proper tables will be required. Mr. Gladstone, I believe, has, or[104] had, three tables in his Temple of Peace—one for correspondence, one for politics, and one for literary work. This, no doubt, is a very excellent plan to be followed by those whose time is precious, and who have to divide each day up for fixed duties. The 'Shannon' and other American tables are very excellent for correspondence work, being fitted with pigeon-holes and drawers, and I have no doubt but that equally well-made tables are made specially fitted for literary work. Such a table should measure not less than six feet by three; its top should be a clear, flat surface, and it should stand firmly on its legs, and these legs should be four, and should not be placed to be in the way of the person sitting at the table. An ink-well should be sunk flush with the top of the case, and it should have a brass cover. A knee-hole table is not the best for literary work, but it may be the best for letter-writing. Of chairs, one good, firm, hard-seated chair is necessary. Mr. Ellwanger[50] says, 'I have two chairs for my reading—a stiff one for books I *have* to read; a luxurious one for books I like to read. My[105] luxurious chair is of dark green leather, a treat to sink into, modelled after the easy armchair of the Eversley Rectory, known from its seductive properties as "Sleepy Hollow."' A very prettily designed and useful hard-seated chair is that known as the Goldsmith chair, being modelled upon the chair which belonged to Oliver Goldsmith. A revolving bookcase is a very appropriate article of furniture in a library. It may be made especially useful for reference-books, or any such books as are being used together at one time for purposes of study and comparison. These revolving bookcases are made in all sizes, and can, of course, be made to suit any particular requirement; thus I have seen them made with a top which can be raised to a slope with a ledge like a standing desk, upon which a large atlas can be rested and consulted. Apart from this, I strongly recommend the use of a standing desk for health's sake when a great deal of writing has to be done.

It frequently happens that books being taken from the shelf, the volumes left behind fall down in an untidy heap. To obviate this, there is a very simple form of metal[106] book support sold, which keeps a half-filled shelf neat and tidy. An alternative to this is the old plan of inserting dummies, whereby no blanks are seen. As I have so strongly advocated shelves the tops of which are within reach of the hand, I need not say much about steps, but where steps are really needed, they should be *very* light, and capable of being easily lifted with one hand. They should have an upright rod support rising about four feet above the top step; this for the purpose of safety when using the steps. Cabinets of drawers for prints and very large books should also be secured if required, and cushioned desks for books with metal bosses or metal mountings of any description. Last, but by no means least, let there be good ink, and plenty of it; good pens, and a variety of them; and good blotting-paper, frequently renewed; and paper-knives of various sizes.

The Library Annexe.

What in many ways is an ideal library is a library housed in a building specially constructed as an annexe to a residence. I feel[107] sure that, within the next ten years, there will be many moderately wealthy men who will be anxious to form libraries and special collections of books, housing them in this way. The idea is only new as applied to large country mansions. Hitherto students of moderate means have managed to construct buildings specially adapted for study and free from interruption. The only instance of a library annexe attached to a country mansion with which I am acquainted is the recent and very notable instance at Hawarden, of which more later. The late Vicar of Middleton Cheney, in Oxfordshire, and, I think, Dr. Jessopp, of Scarning, have both found that their work has been assisted by library annexes. Horace Walpole said of Topham Beauclerk that he had built a library in Great Russell Street, that reached 'half-way to Highgate.' Lord Bacon spent ten thousand pounds in building himself a retreat in his grounds at Gorhambury.

Mr. Gladstone's scheme at Hawarden is likely to be followed by many others. Of course the Hawarden library has been endowed, and made practically open and free. It is the idea of a private library as a[108] temple of peace for the owner and his visitors which we would like to see extended. One fancies that books might be on a better footing in country houses if they had the honour of a separate building. Then they would, at any rate, be on as good a footing as the stables or as the greenhouse, which at present they are not. Books are not so much wall covering, or so much furniture. They are much more; they should be treated more like living creatures, and if only their owners would get upon speaking terms with them, how readily would they get a response. Roughly, then, one would like to see attached to every large country establishment a book building, a centre of intelligence and light, where we might be sure of finding a good atlas, a good biographical dictionary, and good verbal dictionary. I do not understand why so little importance has hitherto been attached to this. Such a building should have a large central room and several separate small rooms for private study. The illustrations in a charming little book called *Mr. Gladstone in the Evening of his Days* convey what is meant very well. From this little volume I give extracts which seem[109] very clear to any one interested in this matter:—

'Everywhere about in the large room are books—books—books. The Iron Library (the building is of iron) is arranged in the same ingenious way as Mr. Gladstone's private library at Hawarden Castle. There are windows on either side of the long room, and between these windows high bookcases, running towards the centre of the room, are put up. There are books on either side of these cases, and the part facing the centre of the room is again arranged to hold books. It is truly marvellous how many books can thus be stored without a single one being out of sight.'

'There is the same simplicity, the same quiet comfort, the same air of repose, and the same absence of library conventionality about. . . . .'

'Through a door . . . . you reach the second room in the library, to which Mr. Gladstone has given the name of the "Humanity room." It is arranged on exactly the same plan as the first, and contains secular works chiefly. You note Madame de Sévigné's *Letters* on one[110] shelf, in neat and dainty little volumes; and yellow-backed Zola lower down.'[51]

Any one who proposed having a library as a separate building should certainly study Mr. Gladstone's experiments at St. Deiniol's Library, or procure *Mr. Gladstone in the Evening of his Days*, wherein are given illustrations of the interior plan and general economy of the structure.[111] Certainly Mr. Gladstone's ideas as to the arrangement of books as put forth in the *Nineteenth Century* for March, 1890, are much more applicable to an annexe library than to the housing of books in an ordinary private dwelling. Thus the arrangement of the bays made by the projections could not be carried out without extensive structural alterations in one house out of twenty in the country, and not one house out of a thousand in London. His ideas, however, are wholly practicable and admirably thorough when applied to the annexe library. It is interesting to see Mr. Gladstone's calculations as to shelf accommodation. They were disputed at the time by some cavilling critics, but have since been shown to be accurate. Mr. Gladstone is speaking[52] of the bookcases round the walls and the projecting arms, and he says:—'I will now exhibit to my readers the practical effect of such arrangement in bringing great numbers of books within easy reach. Let each projection be three feet long, twelve inches deep (ample for two faces of octavos), and nine feet high, so that the upper shelf[112] can be reached by the aid of a wooden stool of two steps, not more than twenty inches high, and portable without the least effort of a single hand. I will suppose the wall-space available to be eight feet, and the projections, three in number, with end pieces, need only put out three feet five, while narrow strips of bookcase will run up the wall between the projections. Under these conditions, the bookcases thus described will carry about 2000 volumes.

'And a library forty feet long and twenty feet broad, amply lighted, having some portion of the centre fitted with very low bookcases, suited to serve for some of the uses of tables, will receive on the floor from 18,000 to 20,000 volumes of all sizes without losing the appearance of a room . . . . while leaving portions of space available near the windows for purposes of study. If a gallery be added, there will be accommodation for a further number of 5000, and the room need be no more than sixteen feet high.'

This estimate of shelf accommodation may be compared with one which was made by Mr. Justin Winsor, the well-known librarian[113] of the Harvard library. He says:—'The book room of the Roxbury branch of the public library of Boston is fifty-three feet long by twenty-seven feet wide, and having three storeys of eight feet each in height will hold 100,000 volumes. . . . . I doubt if any other construction can produce this result.'

The building at Hawarden cost, I believe, 1000*l.*, but whether this is with fittings or not I do not know. It is certain that for men whose books are more numerous than costly the annexe plan is admirable, and the difficulty of excluding damp where four walls are exposed to the elements could surely be overcome. I do not think that Mr. Gladstone makes any mention of iron bookcases, but these are often adopted, and have been made in a very convenient form, particularly that called the Radcliffe iron bookcase, arranged by Sir Henry Acland and Mr. W. Froude. Of this I append a description written by Sir Henry Acland himself.

'The advantages of the bookcase consist in its great stability, in its movability and neatness. It carries 500 average octavo volumes,[114] 250 on either side; it is seven feet high, and stands on any floor space on forty-eight inches by eighteen inches. The cases may stand in any number end to end, or down the centre of a passage, or be placed so as to form squares of any dimensions multiple of the length of the cases, and therefore may enclose studies lined with books, books being also on the outside of the square. When the cases stand end to end they need not be put close to each other, but may have a space in which are shelves of any desired length. Therefore ten iron cases placed in a line, so as to include a space of forty inches between each two cases, will carry the contents of nineteen cases, or 5000 plus 4500 volumes, at the cost of ten cases, plus the wooden shelves of nine. The iron framework costs about 5*l.* 5*s.*, and the wooden shelves about 25*s.* The iron portion will carry only octavos, but the spaces as described above will carry folios, because, to insure stability in the iron frames, diagonal ties run down the centre and divide the shelves into two portions, viz., the two frontages described above. But the stability being ensured in each iron case independently, the intermediate[115] shelves in the spaces may be of the full width of the frames, namely, twenty inches.'[53]

A Librarian.

Until we have more properly trained librarians, it is useless to recommend owners of private libraries to find a librarian, because at present there are very few such men in existence who are properly qualified. A love of books is not enough in a librarian. An orderly mind and great receptive power are most essential. Practical knowledge of bookbinding and a sense of colour are equally essential. He must have no fads of his own to be ever thrusting forward. If he is mad on Geology or Astronomy, he won't do. What, above all, he must know are the sources of information.

A study in the 'Lives' of some of the great librarians would best show what is here meant. Mr. Elton[54] names Antonio Maggliabecchi, the jeweller's shop-boy, who became renowned throughout the world for his abnormal knowledge[116] of books. He never at any time left Florence; but he read every catalogue that was issued, and was in correspondence with all the collectors and librarians of Europe. He was blessed with a prodigious memory, and knew all the contents of a book by 'hunting it with his finger,' or once turning over the pages. He was believed, moreover, to know the habitat of all the rare books in the world; and according to the well-known anecdote he replied to the Grand Duke, who asked for a particular volume: 'The only copy of this work is at Constantinople, in the Sultan's library, the seventh volume in the second bookcase, on the right as you go in.' A similar story was told by Wendell Phillips, the American statesman, about a countryman of his own, George Sumner. An Englishman came to Rome and was anxious to know whether there was in the library of the Pope, the great library of the Vatican, a certain book. . . . . The gentleman went to the Italians that used the library. They referred him to the private secretary of one of the cardinals, and after a moment's thought the secretary answered, 'No, sir, I don't know; but there is a young man in the city from Boston, and if the book is[117] there he will know. They went to George Sumner, and asked him if there was such a volume in the library. 'Yes, it is in the tenth alcove, the third shelf, the seventh book to your right as you enter.'

Similar stories, doubtless, could be told of Bradshaw, the Cambridge University librarian, or of Thomas Ruddiman and George Buchanan.

Mr. Lloyd P. Smith[55] gives the following definition, among others, of the qualifications of a librarian: 'Librarians, like editors and proofreaders, are expected to know everything; and in one sense they should know everything—that is, they should have that *maxima pars eruditionis*, which consists in knowing where everything is to be found. A librarian should be able, of his own knowledge, to answer many questions, and especially the two questions which meet him at every turn, "Where can I find such-and-such information?" and "What is the best work on such-and-such a subject?" These are legitimate questions, which it should be the pride of every librarian to answer offhand .... All the book-learning in the world, however, will be insufficient for the practical[118] duties of his place, unless the librarian has also the organ of order. His motto should be, "A place for everything and everything in its place."'

'The book of regulations for the court and household of Guidobaldo I. contains these rules for the administration of the library:—"The librarian should be learned, of good presence, temper, and manners, correct, and ready of speech. He must get from the gardrobe an inventory of the books, and keep them arranged and easily accessible, whether Latin, Greek, Hebrew, or others, maintaining also the rooms in good condition. He must preserve the books from damp and vermin, as well as from the hands of trifling, ignorant, dirty, and tasteless persons. To those of authority and learning, he ought himself to exhibit them with all facility, courteously explaining their beauty and remarkable characteristics, the handwriting and miniatures, but observant that such abstract no leaves. When ignorant or merely curious persons wish to see them, a glance is sufficient, if it be not some one of considerable influence. When any lock or other requisite is needed, he must take care that it be promptly provided.[119] He must let no book be taken away but by the Duke's orders, and if lent, must get a written receipt, and see to its being returned. When a number of visitors come in, he must be specially watchful that none be stolen. All which is duly seen to by the present courteous and attentive librarian, Messer Agabito."'[56]

The Library Architecturally.

Vitruvius, in his *Architecture*, lays down the rule that libraries ought to face the east, because their use requires the morning light, which will preserve their contents from decay; whereas, if the room should face the south or west, they are liable to be damaged by damp. Mr. J. W. Clark, the very learned historian of the University of Cambridge, commenting on this, says that the first of these considerations did influence early builders, but after the Reformation, when considerations of personal comfort began to be generally accepted, the library could be placed in the position which commanded the greatest amount of warmth. Ancient libraries were never[120] placed on the ground, but usually on the first floor, or even higher, for the sake of preserving their contents from the damp to which ground floors are necessarily subject.[57]

The architect is very frequently a great enemy to the library. Underestimating the amount of wall space likely to be required for the housing of the books, or placing shelves and galleries in such a position that the books are not readily got at. Frequently, too, a country house has no room whatever designed either for study or the reception of books. The entire collection of books should be accessible without steps or ladders. Hot-water pipes should not approach nearer than three feet to the books. Electric light is the best luminant, but gas may safely be used provided there is sufficient ventilation.

The walls, which are towards the outer air, and even the others also, if of brick or stone, ought to be battened.

I have taken from a very excellent book, Kerr's *Gentleman's House*, such ideas and notes as I think are likely to be useful in[121] arranging a library in a country house. Mr. Kerr suggests two plans for a large country house with a library.

'The idea which might first occur to the mind is that of a single spacious apartment; but for convenience and in order to preserve the domestic character, it is generally preferable to make use of several smaller apartments as a *Suite of Libraries*. On this plan the arrangement which is perhaps most favourable to considerations of utility, and on the whole most characteristic, is to set out a given width of clear passage way along the central line of the rooms, and then to divide the space on each side into a succession of compartments or bays, by means of transverse bookcases in pairs back to back; such bays being only large enough to accommodate a reading table with sufficient space around for reaching the books, opening the doors of the cases if any, and so on. If the rooms be lighted from the roof, the lights ought to correspond with the division into compartments, so that none of the fronts of the bookcases shall be placed in shadow. If there be windows in the walls, there ought to be one in each bay along one side of the room or both[122] as may be desired. Bookcases against the walls are obviously most serviceable with the ceiling light; with side windows, even when these are on a high level, there is always a difficulty in reading the back lettering under the light; and when the windows are on a low level, dwarf bookcases under them are practically of little use.

'As for *artistic treatment*, nothing can be more appropriate for the character of a library than those effects which are at the command of the architect in a suite of apartments of this kind, laid out probably with some variety in the general forms as well as in the fittings, and involving perhaps the introduction of sculptures and paintings of a suitable kind. Elaborate effects, however, of whatever sort, and the accommodation of any other works of art than those whose merits are kindred to the character of the more proper contents, ought not to be encouraged.'

A second or alternative plan is a large room with a gallery.

'As regards curiosities and other *artistic or scientific collections*, these may very properly be accommodated, whether in upright cases to[123] correspond with the bookcases, or in cabinets to take the place of the reading tables.

'The arrangements proper for the alternative plan of a large *single library* are obviously simple. A gallery is probably carried round the apartment; the bookcases extend along the wall below and are reproduced above; the light comes either from the roof or the upper part of the walls; the floor area is generally occupied solely by reading tables and cabinets. Objects of art and curiosity, when of large size, are more prominently displayed by this arrangement, and the whole effect may be made very imposing; but it is doubtful whether convenience and comfort can by any means be so properly provided for as in the other model.

'There are questions of detail which might be further entered upon, but a reference to what has already been advanced under the head of the ordinary library will probably suffice.'

In other parts of his excellent manual, Mr. Kerr goes more into detail, and refers to the various general purposes to which a library, as distinct from a study, is put in a country house, as follows:—

'There is a certain standard room which[124] constitutes the library of an average gentleman's house, and the various gradations by which this may be either diminished in importance or augmented are easily understood. It is not a library in the sole sense of a depository for books. There is, of course, the family collection, and the bookcases in which this is accommodated form the chief furniture of the apartment. But it would be an error, except in very special circumstances, to design the library for mere study. It is primarily a sort of morning-room for gentlemen rather than anything else. Their correspondence is done here, their reading, and, in some measure, their lounging; and the billiard-room, for instance, is not unfrequently attached to it. At the same time the ladies are not exactly excluded.

'The *position* of the room internally ought therefore to be in immediate connexion with the principal dwelling rooms, so as to be equally accessible; whilst, on the other hand, as regards external influences, it ought to be kept sufficiently quiet (although this is very seldom a practical problem), to prevent the interruption of reading or writing. In accordance with these general ideas, and bearing out,[125] moreover, the somewhat sober effect which bookcases always produce, the *style* of design and decoration ought to be, although not devoid of cheerfulness, certainly subdued in character.'

As regards aspect, Mr. Kerr is at one with the old Vitruvius already referred to.

'It is not often easy to obtain a choice *aspect* for the library, but whenever this primary pleasantness can be had for it so much the better, and it certainly ought never to be entirely neglected in this respect. The reasons for preferring the south-east in the case of day rooms generally have already been argued; for a library, perhaps, a rather more eastward aspect is better, so that the sun may be off the windows at least before noon; even due east might be preferred by some persons, the sunshine being thus lost about half-past ten. In any case, however, the morning sun is to be preferred to that of midday or afternoon. If the room be large enough *end windows* may be used to advantage here as elsewhere. A *bay window* also is often adopted.

'A difficult question which often arises is how sufficiently to provide for persons engaged[126] in writing a *front light from the left*. It is not that a snug seat by the fireside, with a table conveniently at hand, and a left front light, can by any possibility be provided for many persons at once; but it is very unfortunate when no position whatever will combine these advantages. In a library especially this problem must be well worked out, and not for one writer only, but for several. Ingenuity and perseverance will accomplish wonders, and therefore, with the help of end light, a good library may be expected in this respect to be brought very near perfection.

'The *fireplace* ought to be placed so as to make a good winter fireside, because this is in a measure a sitting-room.

'*Intercommunication* is frequently made with the drawing-room, and sometimes intimately, and this carries with it, no doubt, a certain sort of convenience, because the two rooms can be thrown together occasionally; but it is a question whether, in a good house, and looking at such a question broadly, it is not, on the whole, a serious loss to both rooms as regards their more proper purposes. A door to the dining-room is not formally advisable, nor even one to the[127] gentleman's room, although both these arrangements are to be met with, and are occasionally convenient. A communication with the billiard-room, sometimes made, may give the library too completely the character of a lounge, so as to render it somewhat unfit for its better purposes. When the library of a small house is used as a study, by a clergyman, for instance, or as the business room, a door to the dining-room may be so useful as to be specially admissible, the dining-room being thus brought to serve as a waiting-room for the occasion. The interposition, if possible, of a lobby or small ante-room will, however, be an aid to propriety in almost all these cases.

'It is to be observed that we have been hitherto dealing with the ordinary library of an average house and no more; but when the owner is a man of learning we must either add a *study* or constitute the library itself one. In the latter case, in order to prevent disturbance, the door will be more conveniently placed, not in the main corridor, but indirectly connected therewith. No door of intercommunication ought to connect it with any other room (except[128] possibly the gentleman's room), and the position externally ought to be more than ordinarily secluded. Double doors also may be required. In short, the library, which has hitherto been a public room and somewhat of a lounge, becomes now essentially a private retreat.

'When the books form a *large collection*, and strangers, perhaps, are occasionally admitted for reading or reference, the library necessarily assumes more extensive proportions, and its arrangements become more complicated. For example, heating apparatus becomes very possibly indispensable; the question comes up of ceiling lights; the apartments are probably carried up to the height of two storeys, and galleries formed around. Seclusion becomes again still more a point to be considered.

'The library of the house should also be as comfortable as possible, with broad easy chairs, low centre table for books and periodicals, a large pedestal desk with circular revolving top, to shut up all papers and keep them free from dust. This kind of desk I consider invaluable to any man who really uses his library as a work-room, whether[129] it be for real literary work and study, or for the ordinary examination and arrangement of household accounts; for it is quite impossible, on an ordinary writing table, to keep papers clean or tidy, and this circular-headed desk shuts down at once papers as they lie, which then cannot be "tidied" by the housemaid, who would seem to take a pleasure in putting away papers and notes in all kinds of out-of-the-way corners; the desk should have plenty of drawers and pigeon-holes; these latter, not as many of them are, an inch too narrow or two inches too wide for ordinary letters, but all made for the objects for which they are intended. It may seem absurd to say—think carefully of the use to which the drawers are to be put—but how often are they practically useless or wasteful of precious room, by being made shallower or deeper than is required. The room should be surrounded with bookcases, the lower portion made to take large books, and with some part of it covered in with cupboard fronts, with shelving inside to file away periodicals and papers; the shelf which this lower projection forms will do admirably[130] for the arrangement of ornaments, small busts, or other personal things, with which a man crowds the room he really lives in; of course, I am speaking to those who make a den or working-room of their library, and not to those who fit a back room up with various tiers of shelving, on which are arranged a library of books which are seldom looked at, and where the room is only occasionally used, and that only for the purpose of a cloak-room on grand occasions. Above this lower nest of cupboards and shelving should be shelving arranged for various sizes of books, part carried up all round the room, so as to be within easy reach; the top of these will be found useful for china or busts, or other objects of art, while the centre portions may be carried up to the ceiling to give greater accommodation; all these breaks will take away from the stiffness of the room, and, if properly arranged, will all assist in making the library a room pleasant to work or play in. All this kind of work can be made of plain deal, stained and polished, and is infinitely cheaper than the elaborate movable cases of wainscot or walnut, in[131] which the aim of the designer seems often to make the frame-work as expensive as possible, whereas, in truth, the books within are really what should be thought of and cared for.

'The floor should be painted or stained and varnished all over, so as to be easily cleaned and dusted, and everything that is likely to permanently hold dust should be avoided. On the floor, thus painted, a few cheap Indian or other rugs may be laid about in places where most necessary and useful.

'Too much trouble cannot be taken to make the library a pleasant room to live in; it should have everything arranged and adapted for use and comfort, and not be stiff and dreary with any set arrangement. The panels of the cupboard doors may be filled in with Japanese lacquer-work or painted decoration, and here and there, in the recesses, nests of shelves may be fitted with projecting brackets, designed as part of them, for pieces of china, vases of flowers, or busts, and not looking like bats stuck on to a barn door.

'I must not omit to say that in the lower[132] portion of the bookcase should be arranged drawers—not carried down to the floor, for these are inconvenient—for use for prints and valuable photographs and sketches.

'The library should be essentially home-like, with the wall-space fitted up as conveniently as possible; on the top of the bookcases or nests of shelves, spring roller-blinds might be easily arranged in the cornices to draw down at night or other times, and fasten with clips to protect and preserve the books, &c., within them.

'I might offer many other suggestions for the decoration and furniture of the rooms I have specially referred to. I trust those I have made will be of some practical use, and that, above all, you will believe that my aim throughout has been to avoid all dogmatic and set rules of fashion or design, and to insist only that truth and beauty of form and colour, combined with fitness and common sense, are the main elements of all true artistic treatment in decoration and furniture of modern houses.'[58]

[133]

Munificent Book-buying.

Nordau has estimated that, in England alone, there are from eight hundred to a thousand millionaires, and in Europe altogether, there are at least a hundred thousand persons with fortunes of a million and even more. One could hope that it might be considered a kindness now and then to remind some of these millionaires of certain openings for their money which do not, so far, seem to have occurred to them. Mr. Bernard Shaw not long since pointed out in the *Contemporary Review* an opening whereby an Economic Library might be established, and do great lasting honour to a possible founder. Rich men can always be found to vie with one another in lavish expenditure over a ball or a wedding. Thousands of pounds go for a racehorse and for stable management generally, and the amount we spend upon sports annually is 38,000,000*l.*, or about a pound per head of the population. One hardly likes to say that any sum spent upon sport and outdoor life is too much, but[134] yet this sum is out of proportion. One is jealous of horses and sport, not so much perhaps for the amount spent upon them as much as because one sees that the man who hunts and has racehorses, cares and knows about these things to the extermination of all other interests. Life becomes ill balanced, whereas it is necessary to touch life at many points. 'The strenuous scholar pure and simple,' is becoming more rare, though the type of which the late Mark Pattison was one will never quite die out. But it is not the strenuous *scholar* that one is so anxious to perpetuate, as it is the strenuous and scholarly man of affairs and men of trained ability who have mental muscle for parliamentary work and social problems. Such a class ought to have many recruits from among the wealthier families.

It would assist very much towards this end if men of aptitude were properly trained to act as custodians of books in private houses. The art of knowing how to use books is one which must be learnt, and when properly learnt there is very little indeed that may not be readily found to hand in a library of but small dimensions.[135]

There are, I believe, in England twenty-two packs of staghounds, and 182 packs of foxhounds. As every one of the masters of these packs must be a rich man, I should like to know that he at any rate had a sound copy of the *History* of the county where he hunts; that he had in his smoking room a good Encyclopædia, with fifty other good reference books, and a hundred good novels.

The rich men of old combined patronage of learning with the pomp and splendour of their lives. Lucullus distinguished himself by his vast collection of books, and the liberal access he allowed to lovers of books. 'It was a library,' says Plutarch, 'whose walls, galleries and cabinets were open to all visitors; and the ingenious youths, when at leisure, resorted to this abode of the Muses, to hold literary conversations, in which Lucullus himself loved to join.' The Emperor Augustus was himself an author and a book lover, and called one of his libraries by the name of his sister, Octavia, and the other the temple of Apollo. Tiberius had a library, and Trajan also, and these spent constantly upon their books and the housing of them.[136]

I have taken from Renaissance history pictures of several men who might be taken as types which should exist in every highly civilised country. They have been vividly and admirably pictured by biographers, and one can only hope that the rich men of to-day may in five hundred years' time have as lasting reputations as that of Cosimo, the princely patron of learning, and Niccolo, the man of scholarship and refinement of life.

[137]

PASSAGES ILLUSTRATIVE OF THE FOREGOING.

The Medici and their Friends.

'The chief benefit conferred by Cosimo de' Medici on learning was the accumulation and the housing of large libraries. During his exile he built the library of S. Giorgio Maggiore at Venice, and after his return to Florence he formed three separate collections of MSS. While the hall of the Library of S. Marco was in process of construction, Niccolo de' Niccoli died, in 1437, bequeathing his 800 MSS., valued at 6000 golden florins, to sixteen trustees. Among these were Cosimo and Lorenzo de' Medici, Ambrogio Traversari, Lionardo Bruni, Carlo Marsuppini, Poggio Bracciolini, Giannozzo Manetti, and Franco Sachetti. At the same time the estate of Niccolo was compromised by heavy debts. These debts Cosimo cancelled, obtaining in exchange the right to dispose of the library. In 1441 the hall of the convent was finished. Four hundred of Niccolo's MSS. were placed there, with this inscription upon each: *Ex hereditate doctissimi viri Nicola de Nicolis de Florentiâ.* Tommasso Parentucelli made a catalogue at Cosimo's[138] request, in which he not only noted the titles of Niccoli's books, but also marked the names of others wanting to complete the collection. This catalogue afterwards served as a guide to the founders of the libraries of Fiesole, Urbino, and Pesaro, and was, says Vespasiano, indispensable to book-collectors. Of the remaining 400 volumes Cosimo kept some for his own (the Medicean) library, and some he gave to his friends. At the same time he spared no pains to buy codices, while Vespasiano and Fra Giuliano Lapaccini were employed in copying rare MSS. As soon as Cosimo had finished building the Abbey of Fiesole, he set about providing this also with a library suited to the wants of learned ecclesiastics. Of the method he pursued, Vespasiano, who acted as his agent, has transmitted the following account:—"One day when I was in his room, he said to me, 'What plan can you recommend for the formation of this library?' I answered that to buy the books would be impossible, since they could not be purchased. 'What, then, do you propose?' he added. I told him that they must be copied. He then asked if I would undertake the business. I replied that I was willing. He bade me begin at my leisure, saying that he left all to me; and for the monies wanted day by day, he ordered that Don Arcangelo, at that time prior of the monastery, should draw cheques upon his bank, which should be honoured. After beginning the collection, since it was his will that it should be finished with all speed possible, and money was not lacking, I soon engaged forty-five copyists, and in twenty-two months provided[139] two hundred volumes, following the admirable list furnished by Pope Nicholas V.'"[59]

'Cosimo's zeal for learning was not confined to the building of libraries or to book collecting. His palace formed the centre of a literary and philosophical Society, which united all the wits of Florence and the visitors who crowded to the capital of culture. Vespasiano states that "he was always the father and benefactor of those who showed any excellence." Distinguished by versatility of tastes and comprehensive intellect, he formed his own opinion of the men of eminence with whom he came in contact, and conversed with each upon his special subject. When giving audience to the scholars, he discoursed concerning letters; in the company of theologians he showed his acquaintance with theology, a branch of learning always studied by him with delight. So also with regard to philosophy. Astrologers found him well versed in their science, for he somewhat lent faith to astrology, and employed it on certain private occasions. Musicians in like manner perceived his mastery of music, wherein he much delighted. The same was true about sculpture and painting: both of these arts he understood completely, and showed great favour to all worthy craftsmen. In architecture he was a consummate judge, for without his opinion and advice no building was begun or carried to completion.'[60]

[140]

'Never was there a time in the world's history when money was spent more freely upon the collection and preservation of MSS. and when a more complete machinery was put in motion for the sake of securing literary treasures. Prince vied with prince, and eminent burgher with burgher, in buying books. The commercial correspondents of the Medici and other great Florentine houses, whose banks and discount offices extended over Europe and the Levant, were instructed to purchase relics of antiquity without regard for cost, and to forward them to Florence. The most acceptable present that could be sent to a king was a copy of a Roman Historian.'[61]

'Among the friends of Cosimo, to whose personal influences at Florence the Revival of Learning owed a vigorous impulse, Niccolo de' Niccoli claims our attention. . . . . His judgment in matters of style was so highly valued that it was usual for scholars to submit their essays to his eyes before they ventured upon publication. . . . . Notwithstanding his fine sense of language, Niccolo never appeared before the world of letters as an author. . . . Certainly his reserve in an age noteworthy for display has tended to confer on him distinction. The position he occupied at Florence was that of a literary dictator. All who needed his assistance and advice were received with urbanity. He threw his house open to young men of parts, engaged in disputations with the curious, and provided the ill-educated with teachers.[141] Foreigners from all parts of Europe paid him visits. The strangers who came to Florence at that time, if they missed the opportunity of seeing him at home, thought they had not been in Florence. The house where he lived was worthy of his refined taste and cultivated judgment, for he had formed a museum of antiquities—inscriptions, marbles, coins, vases, and engraved gems. There he not only received students and strangers, but conversed with sculptors and painters, discussing their inventions as freely as he criticised the essays of the scholars..... Vespasiano's account of his personal habits presents so vivid a picture that I cannot refrain from translating it at length:—"First of all, he was of a most fair presence; lively, for a smile was ever on his lips, and very pleasant in his talk. He wore clothes of the fairest crimson cloth, down to the ground. He never married, in order that he might not be impeded in his studies. A housekeeper provided for his daily needs. He was, above all men, the most cleanly in eating, as also in all other things. When he sat at table, he ate from fair antique vases, and, in like manner, all his table was covered with porcelain and other vessels of great beauty. The cup from which he drank was of crystal, or of some other precious stone. To see him at table—a perfect model of the men of old—was of a truth a charming sight. He always willed that the napkins set before him should be of the whitest, as well as all the linen." .... What distinguished Niccolo was the combination of refinement and humane breeding with open-handed generosity and devotion to the cause of culture. He knew how to[142] bring forward men of promise and place them in positions of eminence.'[62]

'Lorenzo attracted to his villa the greatest scholars and most brilliant men of the time, a circle which included Poliziano, Landino, Ficino, Pico della Mirandola, Alberti, Pulci, and Michael Angelo. The interests of this circle, as of all similar Italian circles of the time, were largely absorbed in the philosophy and literature of Greece, and special attention was devoted to the teachings of Plato. Plato's writings were translated into Latin by Ficino, and the translation was printed in 1482, at the cost of Filippo Valvio. Ficino was too poor himself to undertake the publication of his works, and this was the case with not a few of the distinguished authors of the age. The presentation of books to the public required at this time what might be called the endowment of literature, and endowment which was supplied by the liberality of wealthy patrons possessed of literary appreciation or public-spirited ambition, or of both. As Symonds expresses it, "Great literary undertakings involved in that century the substantial assistance of wealthy men, whose liberality was rewarded by a notice in the colophon or in the title-page." The formal dedication was an invention of a somewhat later date.'[63]

'Of Palla degli Strozzi's services in the cause of Greek learning I have already spoken. Beside the[143] invitation which he caused to be sent to Manuel Chrysoloras, he employed his wealth and influence in providing books necessary for the prosecution of Hellenic studies. "Messer Palla," says Vespasiano, "sent to Greece for countless volumes, all at his own cost. The *Cosmography* of Ptolemy, together with the picture made to illustrate it, the *Lives* of Plutarch, the works of Plato, and very many other writings of philosophers, he got from Constantinople. The *Politics* of Aristotle were not in Italy until Messer Palla sent for them; and when Messer Lionardo of Arezzo translated them, he had the copy from his hands." In the same spirit of practical generosity Palla degli Strozzi devoted his leisure and his energies to the improvement of the *studio pubblico* at Florence, giving it that character of humane culture which it retained throughout the age of the Renaissance. To him, again, belongs the glory of having first collected books for the express purpose of founding a public library. This project had occupied the mind of Petrarch, and its utility had been recognised by Coluccio de' Salutati, but no one had as yet arisen to accomplish it. "Being passionately fond of literature, Messer Palla always kept copyists in his own house and outside it, of the best who were in Florence, both for Greek and Latin books; and all the books he could find he purchased, on all subjects, being minded to found a most noble library in Santa Trinità, and to erect there a most beautiful building for the purpose. He wished that it should be open to the public, and he chose Santa Trinità because it was in the centre of Florence, a site of great convenience[144] to everybody. His disasters supervened and what he had designed he could not execute."'[64]

'Cosimo used to regret that "he had not begun to spend money upon public works ten years earlier than he did." Every costly building that bore his name, each library he opened to the public, and all the donations lavished upon scholars, served the double purpose of cementing the despotism of his house and of gratifying his personal enthusiasm for culture. . . . . Of his generosity to men of letters, the most striking details are recorded. When Niccolo de' Niccoli ruined himself, Cosimo opened for him an unlimited credit with the Medicean bank.'[65]

The Dukes of Urbino.

'Mr. Roscoe has observed that "by no circumstance in the character of an individual is the love of literature so strongly evinced as by the propensity for collecting together the writings of illustrious scholars, and compressing the 'soul of ages past' within the narrow limits of a library." But it is not easy now to appreciate the obstacles attending such a pursuit in the age of Federigo. The science of bibliography can scarcely be said to have existed before the invention of printing, in consequence of the extreme difficulty of becoming acquainted with works of which there were but few copies, and these widely scattered, perhaps scarcely known. Great outlay was required,[145] either to search out or transcribe manuscripts, and even the laborious habits which then accompanied learning shrank from a task so beset by obstructions. Yet there was a bright exception in Thomas of Saranza, whose learning supplied the knowledge, and whose elevation to the triple tiara as Nicholas V. procured him the opportunities necessary for amassing a library. Not only did he found that of the Vatican, but he prepared for Cosimo, *Pater patrie*, a list of authors for the infant collection of S. Marco, at Florence, which, being recognised as a standard catalogue, was adopted by Count Federigo. The longer life allowed to the latter enabled him to outstrip these bibliomaniacs, and all contemporary accumulators, until the fame of his library stood unrivalled. Accordingly Ruscelli, in his *Imprese Illustri*, avers it to be "notorious that the earliest and most famous collection formed out of the ruins of antiquity was that of Urbino, from whence many excellent authors were edited, and copies supplied."'[66]

'In no respect did he look to expense; and whenever he learned the existence of any desirable book in Italy, or abroad, he sent for it without heeding the cost. His librarian, Vespasiano, wrote, "It is now above fourteen years since he began to make this collection, and he has ever since at Urbino, Florence, and elsewhere, thirty-four transcribers, and has resorted to every means requisite for amassing a famous and excellent library."'[67]

[146]

'To the right and left of the carriage entrance into the great courtyard, are two handsome saloons, each about forty-five feet by twenty-two, and twenty-three in height. That on the left contained the famous library of manuscripts collected by Count Federigo; the corresponding one received the printed books, which, gradually purchased by successive dukes, became under the last sovereign, a copious collection. Baldi, in his description of the palace, printed in Bianchini's work, dwells on the judicious adaptation of the former, its windows set high against the northern sky, admitting a subdued and steady light which invited to study; its air cool in summer, temperate in winter; its walls conveniently shelved; the character and objects of the place fittingly set forth in a series of rude hexameters inscribed on the cornices. Adjoining was a closet fitted up with inlaid and gilded panelling, beneath which Timoteo della Vite, a painter whose excellence we shall attest in our thirtieth chapter, depicted Minerva with her ægis, Apollo with his lyre, and the nine muses with their appropriate symbols. A similar small study was fitted up immediately over this one, set round with arm-chairs encircling a table, all mosaicked with *tarsia*, and carved by Maestro Giacomo of Florence, while on each compartment of the panelling was the portrait of some famous author, and an appropriate distich. One other article of furniture deserves special notice—a magnificent eagle of gilt bronze, serving as a lectern in the centre of the manuscript room. It was carried to Rome at the devolution of the duchy to the Holy See, but was rescued by Pope[147] Clement XI. from the Vatican library, and restored to his native town, where it has long been used in the choir of the cathedral.'[68]

'Of Francesco Maria's literary pursuits we have various pleasing memorials. Not satisfied with the valuable library of MSS. that had descended to him from the Feltrian dukes, he formed another of standard printed works. Indeed, he became an assiduous book-collector; and the letters of his librarian, Benedetto Benedetti, in the Oliveriana Library, are full of lists which his agents in Venice, Florence, and even Frankfort are urged to supply. In his own voluminous correspondence, we find constant offers from authors of dedications or copies of their productions, the tone of which is highly complimentary to his taste for letters. In 1603, the Archbishop of Monreale, in Spain, transmits him the regulations he proposed to prescribe in bequeathing his library to a seminary he had founded in his diocese, expressing a hope that they might prove useful to the Duke's collection, "at this moment without parallel in the world." Instead of quoting the vague testimony of courtly compliment, as to the use which this philosophic Prince made of these acquisitions, let us cite the brief records of his studies, preserved in his own Diary. In 1585, "terminated an inspection of the whole works of Aristotle, on which I have laboured no less than fifteen years, having had them generally read to me by Maestro Cesare Benedetti, of Pesaro.'"[69]

[148]

'Francesco di Giorgio, in his *Treatise on Architecture*, mentions Duke Federigo as holding out inducements for the learned men at his court to illustrate the works of classic authors on architecture and sculpture. But no testimony to his literary habits can be more satisfactory than that of his librarian, Vespasiano, to the following purpose. The Duke was a ready Latin scholar, and extremely fond of ancient history. As a logician he had attained considerable aptitude, having studied Aristotle's *Ethics* along with Maestro Lazzaro, a famous theologian, who became Bishop of Urbino, discussing with him the most intricate passages. By the like process he mastered the Stagirite's politics, physics, and other treatises; and having acquired more philosophy than any contemporary prince, his thirst for new sources of knowledge induced him to devote himself to theology with equal zeal. The principal works of St. Thomas Aquinas and Duns Scotus were habitually read to him; he preferred the former as more clear, but admitted that the latter displayed more subtlety in argument. He was well acquainted with the Bible, as well as the commentaries of Saints Ambrose, Jerome, Augustine, and Gregory; also with the writings of the Greek fathers, such as Saints Basil, Chrysostom, Gregory Naziazen, Nicetas, Athanasius, and Cyril. Among the classic authors whom he was in the habit of reading or listening to were Livy, Sallust, Quintus Curtius, Justin, Cæsar, Plutarch, Ælius Spartianus, Æmylius Protus, Tacitus, Suetonius, Eusebius. All men of letters visiting Urbino were hospitably entertained, and several[149] were always attached to his court. His largesses to such were at all times liberal. He spent above 1500 ducats in this way when at Florence, and remitted similar bounties to Rome and Naples. He gave 1000 ducats to the learned Campano, professor of belles-lettres at Perugia in 1455, who aided him in collecting ancient MSS., and became Bishop of Teramo.'[70]

Pieresc.

'When any library was to be sold by public outcry, he took care to buy the best books, especially if they were of some neat edition that he did not already possess. He bound his books in red morocco, with his cypher or initials in gold. One binder always lived in the house, and sometimes several were employed at once "when the books came rolling in on every side."' 'Your house and library' (says the dedication of a book to Pieresc) 'are a firmament wherein the stars of learning shine; the desks are lit with starlight, and the books are in constellations, and you sit like the sun in the midst, embracing and giving light to them all.' 'The library is to be open to all the world without the exception of any living soul; readers were to be supplied with chairs and writing materials, and the attendants will fetch all books required in any language or department of learning, and will change them as often as is necessary.'[71]

[150]

'Bouchard states, in his funeral oration on Pieresc, "To this his shop and storehouse of wisdom and virtue, Peireskius did not only courteously admit all travellers, studious of art and learning, opening to them all the treasures of his library, but he would keep them there a long time, with free and liberal entertainment; and at their departure, would give them books, coins, and other things, which seemed most suitable to their studies; also he freely gave them at his own expense, whatever things they wanted, most liberally, even as to all other learned men, who were absent, and whose names he had only heard of; whatever he had among his books or relics of antiquity, which he thought might assist them in their writings, he would send it them of his own accord, not only without their desiring the same, but many times when they were ignorant of such things.'[72]

Mr. Ruskin's Advice.

'I say first we have despised literature. What do we, as a nation, care about books? How much do you think we spend altogether on our libraries, public or private, as compared with what we spend on our horses? If a man spends lavishly on his library, you call him mad—a biblio-maniac. But you never call any one a horse maniac, though men ruin themselves every day by their horses, and you do not hear of people ruining themselves by their books. Or, to go lower still, how much do you think the bookshelves of the[151] United Kingdom, public and private, would fetch, as compared with the contents of its wine-cellars? What position would its expenditure on literature take as compared with its expenditure on luxurious eating? We talk of food for the mind, as of food for the body: now a good book contains such food inexhaustibly; it is a provision for life, and for the best part of us; yet how long most people would look at the best book before they would give the price of a large turbot for it!'[73]

'It will be long yet before that comes to pass. Nevertheless, I hope it will not be long before royal or national libraries will be founded in every considerable city, with a royal series of books in them; the same series in every one of them, chosen books, the best in every kind, prepared for that national series in the most perfect way possible; their text printed all on leaves of equal size, broad of margin, and divided into pleasant volumes, light in the hand, beautiful and strong, and thorough as examples of binder's work.'[73]

'I could shape for you other plans, for art galleries and for natural history galleries, and for many precious, many, it seems to me, needful things; but this book plan is the easiest and needfullest, and would prove a considerable tonic to what we call our British constitution, which has fallen dropsical of late, and has an evil thirst, and evil hunger, and wants healthier feeding. You have got its Corn Laws repealed for it; try if you cannot get Corn Laws established for it dealing in a better bread—bread made of that old[152] enchanted Arabian grain, the Sesame, which opens doors, doors, not of robbers', but of kings' treasuries.'[74]

'Whatever the hold which the aristocracy of England has on the heart of England, in that they are still always in front of her battles, this hold will not be enough, unless they are also in front of her thoughts.'[75]

'But it is not gold that you want to gather! What is it? Greenbacks? No; not those neither. What is it then—is it ciphers after a capital I? Cannot you practise writing ciphers, and write as many as you want? Write ciphers for an hour every morning, in a big book, and say every evening, I am worth all those noughts more than I was yesterday. Won't that do? Well, what in the name of Plutus is it you want? Not gold, not greenbacks, not ciphers after a capital I? You will have to answer after all, "No; we want, somehow or other, money's *worth*." Well, what is that? Let your Goddess of Getting-on discover it, and let her learn to stay therein.'[76]

'And the entire object of true education is to make people not merely *do* the right things, but *enjoy* the right things—not merely industrious, but to love industry—not merely learned, but to love knowledge—not merely pure, but to love purity—not merely just, but to hunger and thirst after justice.'[77]

[153]

FOOTNOTES:

[1] Stevens' *Who spoils our English Books?*

[2] Stevens' *Who spoils our English Books?*

[3] Blades' *Enemies of Books* (p. 25).

[4] Ellwanger's *Story of my House*, p. 213.

[5] D. Clement, *Bibliothèque curieuse*.

[6] Edwards, *Memoirs of Libraries*, ii. 647-649.

[7] Edwards, ii. 659.

[8] Leighton (John), *Book-plate Annual*.

[9] *Enemies of Books*.

[10] P. G. Hamerton.

[11] P. G. Hamerton.

[12] H. W. Beecher.

[13] James Payn.

[14] *Blackwood's Magazine*, February, 1896.

[15] *Blackwood's Magazine*, February, 1896.

[16] Burke.

[17] Thirlwall.

[18] *Blackwood's Magazine*, February, 1896.

[19] J. S. Blackie.

[20] H. D. Traill.

[21] See Mr. Gladstone's ideas on the subject, in *Gladstone in the Evening of his Days*, p. 145.

[22] Bowen's lecture on *Novel Reading*.

[23] 'Periodically I am addressed by two constant and somewhat exigeant classes of correspondents: the young gentlemen who wish me to give them a list of the works requisite to form a journalist's library; and, next, the esteemed individuals of both sexes and all ages who want me to tell them how to keep a commonplace-book. I have replied to both these questions over and over again; and to give yet another list of the books which I think would be useful to professional writers for the press would be to outrage the patience of my non-professional patrons. The recipe for keeping a commonplace-book may, however, it is to be hoped, be repeated without giving offence to any one. Here it is; and pray observe that I have had it printed in small type, in order that the susceptibilities of readers who want to be amused and do not require to be instructed may not be wounded:—Procure a blank book, strongly bound, big or little, according to the largeness or smallness of your handwriting. Let the book have an index. It will be better if the paper of the book were ruled. When in the course of your reading you come on a passage which strikes you as worthy of being common-placed, copy it legibly in your commonplace-book. Say that the passage is the following, from Bacon's *Natural History:* "So the beard is younger than the hair of the head, and doth, for the most part, wax hoary later." At the end of this passage inscribe a circle or an ellipse, a square or a lozenge, just as you choose to do; and in the inscribed space write with red ink (better still with carmine) the figure 1. Then index the passage under letter B. "Beard younger than hair of head. 1." If you wish to be very careful in your common-placing, you may double index the passage by turning to letter H, and indicating the passage as "Head, hair of, older than beard." And so you may continue to transcribe consecutively all the passages which strike you in the course of your reading: never omitting to number the passage and to index it as soon as numbered. That is the system adopted by the Distressed Compiler, and he has made constant use of it for nearly forty years.'—G. A. SALA.

[24] Those who read everything acquire something, and especially they acquire, as the Bishop of Oxford (Dr. Wilberforce), once said, the invaluable power of knowing where, when they wanted first-hand information, they could most easily obtain it. That is the knowledge of the lawyer; and the knowledge of the lawyer, if he is competent, gradually becomes of the kind which qualifies him to be a judge.—*Spectator*, January 2nd, 1897.

[25] Napoleon was a great lover of small books. 'An insatiate reader while on his travels, Napoleon complained, when at Warsaw, in 1807, and when at Bayonne, in 1808, that his librarian at Paris did not keep him well supplied with books. "The Emperor," wrote the secretary to Barbier, "wants a portable library of a thousand volumes in 12mo., printed in good type without margin, and composed as nearly as possible of forty volumes on religion, forty of epics, forty of plays, sixty of poetry, a hundred of novels, sixty of history, the remainder, to make up the thousand, of historical memoirs. The religious works are to be the Old and New Testament, the Koran, a selection of the works of the Fathers of the Church, works respecting the Aryans, Calvinists, of Mythology, &c. The epics are to be Homer, Lucan, Tasso, Telemachus, The Henriade, &c." Machiavelli, Fielding, Richardson, Montesquieu, Voltaire, Corneille, Racine, and Rousseau were also among the authors mentioned.'

[26] *Murray's Magazine*, September, 1889.

[27] *Nineteenth Century*, January, 1884.

[28] Parker, *Domestic Architecture*.

[29] Putnam, *Books and their Makers*, vol. i.

[30] See *ante*, p. 8.

[31] Many interesting references to Pepys' Collections are found in Mr. H. B. Wheatley's *Pepys, and the World he Lived in*. The following extracts are taken from the same writer's new and final edition of the *Diary*:—

May 15, 1660.—'After that to a bookseller's and bought for the love of the binding three books: the French *Psalms* in four parts, Bacon's *Organon*, and Farnab. *Rhetor.*'[32]

Dec. 26, 1662.—'Hither come Mr. Battersby; and we falling into a discourse of a new book of drollery in verse called *Hudebras*,[33] I would needs go find it out, and met with it at the Temple: cost me 2*s.* 6*d.*'

July 8, 1664.—'So to Paul's Churchyarde about my books, and to the binder's, and directed the doing of my *Chaucer*,[34] though they were not full neate enough for me, but pretty well it is; and thence to the clasp-maker's to have it clasped and bossed.'

Jan. 18, 1664-65.—'Up and by and by to my bookseller's, and there did give thorough direction for the new binding of a great many of my old books, to make my whole study of the same binding, within very few.'

Aug. 24, 1666.—'Up, and despatched several businesses at home in the morning, and then comes Sympson to set up my other new presses[35] for my books, and so he and I fell into the furnishing of my new closett, and taking out the things out of my old, and I kept him with me all day, and he dined with me, and so all the afternoon till it was quite dark hanging things, that is my maps and pictures and draughts, and setting up my books, and as much as we could do, to my most extraordinary satisfaction.'

Dec. 17, 1666.—'Spent the evening in fitting my books, to have the number set upon each, in order to my having an alphabet of my whole, which will be of great ease to me. This day Captain Batters come from sea in his fireship and come to see me, poor man, as his patron, and a poor painful wretch he is as can be. After supper to bed.'

Dec. 19, 1666.—'Home full of trouble on these considerations, and, among other things, I to my chamber, and there to ticket a good part of my books, in order to the numbering of them for my easy finding them to read as I have occasion.'

Jan. 8, 1666-67.—'So home and to supper, and then saw the catalogue of my books, which my brother had wrote out, now perfectly alphabeticall, and so to bed.'

Feb. 4, 1666-67.—'Mightily pleased with the play, we home by coach, and there a little to the office, and then to my chamber, and there finished my catalogue of my books with my own hand, and so to supper and to bed, and had a good night's rest, the last night's being troublesome, but now my heart light and full of resolution of standing close to my business.'

Feb. 8, 1667-68.—'Thence away to the Strand, to my bookseller's, and there staid an hour, and bought the idle, rogueish book, *L'escholle des filles*, which I have bought in plain binding, avoiding the buying of it better bound, because I resolve, as soon as I have read it, to burn it, that it may not stand in the list of books, nor among them, to disgrace them if it should be found. Thence home, and busy late at the office, and then home to supper and to bed.'

[32] *Index Rhetoricus*, of Thomas Farnaby, was a book which went through several editions. The first was published at London, by R. Allot, in 1633.

[33] The first edition of Butler's *Hudibras* is dated 1663, and it probably had only been published a few days when Pepys bought it and sold it at a loss. He subsequently endeavoured to appreciate the work, but was not successful. The edition in the Pepysian Library is dated 1689.

[34] This was Speght's edition of 1602, which is still in the Pepysian Library. The book is bound in calf, with brass clasps and bosses. It is not lettered.

[35] These presses still exist, and, according to Pepys' wish, they are placed in the second court of Magdalene College, in a room which they exactly fit, and the books are arranged in the presses just as they were when presented to the college.

[36] *Tatler*, No. 158.

[37] Wheatley, *Pepys and the World he Lived in*, p. 84.

[38] I believe these rules were originally drawn up by Mr. B. R. Wheatley.

[39] No bookshelves ought to be beyond the reach of a moderately tall person.

[40] 'The books were numbered consecutively throughout the library, and, therefore, when rearranged, they needed all to be renumbered. All hands were pressed into this service, and we read that on the 15th of February, 1667-68, Pepys himself, his wife, and Deb. Willett were busy until near midnight "titleing" the books for the year, and setting them in order. They all tired their backs, but the work was satisfactory..... (See *ante*, p. 78.)

'The books are arranged in eleven curious old mahogany bookcases, which are mentioned in the *Diary* under date August 24, 1666. "Up and dispatched several businesses at home in the morning, and then comes Sympson to set up my other new presses for my books, and so he and I fell into the furnishing of my new closett, and taking out the things out of my old, and I kept him with me all day, and he dined with me, and so all the afternoon till it was quite darke hanging things, that is, my maps and pictures and draughts, and setting up my books, ... to my most extraordinary satisfaction."'—Wheatley, *Pepys and the World he lived in*, pp. 83-4.

[41] *Library Journal*, August, 1878.

[42] Tonks' fittings are specially adapted for the shelves of book-cases or other shelves, the adjustment of which has, from time to time, to be varied to suit the varying requirements of a library, &c. The method

hitherto generally adopted for such shelves is to support them at each end by two studs, the heads of which are mortised into the shelf, and the pins driven or otherwise fitted into holes two or more inches apart, bored in two rows into the upright frames; these holes are very seldom accurately fitted to the pins, and even where so done in the first instance, from the shrinking or expansion of the wood, they soon become too large or too small for the pins, and the alteration of the adjustment of a shelf is thereby rendered an extremely troublesome operation. The patent fittings remedy this, and save both time and trouble; in place of the rows of holes so far apart, metal strips perforated at intervals of three-quarters of an inch for the reception of the very simple but strong metal plates, which take the place of the old studs, are mortised in and screwed to the frames. The insertion, at the required intervals, of the plates into the perforations in these strips is made instantaneously, consequently the position of a shelf can be easily altered without an irritating expense of trouble, and waste of time. The thinness of the plates renders any mortising in the shelf unnecessary, and the small intervals between the perforations in the strips enables the whole space occupied by the shelves to be used most economically. These fittings, when used with a shelf sufficiently strong itself to bear the weight, will support without strain more than half a ton.

[43] *Nineteenth Century*, March, 1890.

[44] Edwards, *Memoirs of Libraries*, ii., 736.

[45] THE SIZES OF BOOKS.—The Associated Librarians of Great Britain decided upon a uniform and arbitrary scale for the measurement and description of the sizes of books. In consequence of the many and varied sizes of papers now manufactured, the terms folio, quarto or 4to., octavo or 8vo., twelvemo or 12mo., and so on, as indicating the number of folds in the printed sheets, can no longer be relied upon as a definite guide to the sizes of books, hence the change, as follows:—

Large folio	la. fol.	over	18 inches.
Folio	fol.	below	18 "
Small folio	sm. fol.	"	13 "
Large octavo	la. 8vo.	"	11 "
Octavo	8vo.	"	9 "
Small octavo	sm. 8vo.	"	8 "
Duodecimo	12mo.	"	8 "

Decimo octavo	18mo.	is	6	"
Minimo	mo.	below	6	"
Large quarto	la. 4to.	"	15	"
Quarto	4to.	"	11	"
Small quarto	sm. 4to.	"	8	"

[46] Edwards, *Memoirs of Libraries*, ii., 739.

[47] Blades, *Enemies of Books*.

[48] Edwards, ii., 737.

[49] See p. 106.

[50] *The Story of my House*.

[51] These notices of the Hawarden Library may be compared with the accounts given in Dennistoun's *Dukes of Urbino* of a great Florentine library:—

'Adjoining (the main library) was a study, fitted up with inlaid and gilded panelling, beneath which .... were depicted Minerva with her ægis, Apollo with his lyre, and the nine muses, with their appropriate symbols. A similar small study was fitted up immediately over this one, set round with armchairs encircling a table, all mosaicked with *tarsia*, ... while in each compartment of the panelling was the portrait of some famous author, and an appropriate distich. ... To the right and left of the carriage entrance into the great courtyard are two handsome saloons, each about forty-five feet by twenty-two, and twenty-three in height. That on the left contained the famous library of MS. collected by Count Federigo; the corresponding one received the printed books which, gradually purchased by successive dukes, became, under the last sovereign a copious collection. Baldi, in his description of the palace, printed in Bianchini's works, dwells on the judicious adaptation of the former, its windows set high against the northern sky, admitting a subdued and steady light which invited to study; its air cool in summer, temperate in winter; its walls conveniently sheltered. . . . .'

[52] *Nineteenth Century*, March, 1890.

[53] *Library Assoc. Report*, 1878, p. 75.

[54] *Great Book Collectors*, p. 74.

[55] *American Library Journal*, vol. i., p. 69.

[56] *Memoirs of the Dukes of Urbino*, p. 159.

[57] Willis and Clark, *History of Cambridge University*, vol. iii., p. 416.

[58] Edis, *Decoration and Furniture of Town Houses*, pp. 188-191.

[59] Symonds, *The Revival of Learning*, pp. 174, 175.

[60] *Ibid.*, pp. 172-7.

[61] Symonds, *Revival of Learning*, pp. 139, 140.

[62] Symonds, *Revival of Learning*, pp. 180-2.

[63] Putnam, *Books and their Makers*, vol. i., p. 338.

[64] Symonds, *Revival of Learning*, p. 167.

[65] *Ibid.*, pp. 172-3.

[66] Dennistoun, *Memoirs of the Dukes of Urbino*, vol. i., p. 155.

[67] *Ibid.*, vol. i., pp. 156-7.

[68] *Memoirs of the Dukes of Urbino*, vol. i., pp. 153-5.

[69] *Ibid.*, vol. i., p. 154.

[70] *Memoirs of the Dukes of Urbino*, pp. 219, 220.

[71] Elton, *Great Book Collectors*, pp. 180-4.

[72] *The Library*, July, 1895.

[73] *Sesame and Lilies*.

[74] *Sesame and Lilies*.

[75] *Crown of Wild Olive*, p. 87.

[76] *Ibid.*, p. 60.

[77] *Ibid.*, p. 46.

Milton Keynes UK
Ingram Content Group UK Ltd.
UKHW042348121024
449589UK00004B/318